BOSNIAN-ENGLISH/ENGLISH-BOSNIAN DICTIONARY AND PHRASEBOOK

BOSNIAN-ENGLISH/ENGLISH-BOSNIAN DICTIONARY AND PHRASEBOOK

by
Susan Kroll and Dževad Zahirović

with assistance from
Zumreta Zahirović,
Elvir and "Jackie" Jandrić,
and Sanel Valjevac

HIPPOCRENE BOOKS
New York

I would like to thank the Zahirović family for all their help and support in making this book. I could not have done it without them. I would also like to acknowledge Elvir and "Jackie" Jandrić, and Sanel Valjevac for their help and patience.

This book is dedicated to my first Bosnian teachers and dear friends in Banovići: Nataša, Amela, Enver, and Nedim; and my adopted family: Bajro, Najla, Samira, Elvis, Samir, Seki, Mirsada, and Vanesa "Ginger". Within all of you lies the hope of your country, and I am deeply grateful that you took me into your heart. I wish you peace and justice.

Fourth printing, 2006.

Copyright© 1998 Susan Kroll.

For information, address:
HIPPOCRENE BOOKS, INC.
171 Madison Avenue
New York, NY 10016

Cataloging-in-Publication Data available from the Library of Congress

ISBN 0-7818-0596-1

Printed in the United States of America.

Table of Contents

Foreword

Although the purpose of this book is to facilitate
communication, I'm afraid I am further cementing the
divisions among the people of former-Yugoslavia.
Where there was once one country and one language
with many dialects, there are now many languages, of
which Bosnian is one. Bosnian is a language in the
making. Those who were persecuted by the Serbians
want to differentiate their language by using the
Croatian forms, while those harassed by the Croatians
prefer the Serbian forms of words. There is also a push
to capture the unique Bosnian accent by putting extra *ij*s
in words, and also a search for the old Turkish phrases.
The people who have helped me with this book could
not agree among themselves on which was the correct
spelling; and people using this book will come across
words considered mistakes by Bosnians in different parts
of the country. I have tried to obtain information from
people from various areas to minimize this problem, but
I know it still exists

Preface

This is a book for people who want to speak
Bosnian. Using this book will help you get
your message across and understand what is
being said to you. Don't worry about speaking
perfectly (Bosnian grammar can prove daunting
to English speakers). My experience is that the
Bosnian people are very patient and will
forgive your mistakes as long as you are willing
to try! I'd like to encourage everyone working
in or visiting Bosnia to be able to communicate
with the local people. I'm sure that you will
find that to be the highlight of your stay. That
is what this book is all about. So get out there
and start talking!

Susan Kroll

Pronunciation Guide

English speakers will have problems with this because there are no silent letters, no fancy tricks, and no exceptions!! And we just can't get used to that...

Vowels

a	as in ah!
e	as in best
i	as in need
o	as in okay
u	as in moon

Sometimes you will see words devoid of vowels - but that is because sometimes r is a vowel! So imagine an e in front of the r and you will be able to say it: *vrt* (garden) is pronounced "vert." Feel free to roll the r a little.

Some cool **consonants** that we don't have are:
ć, č--which is a hard ch and a soft ch sound, but to us they sound the same
đ, dž--is j like in jay--again, we can't tell the difference between them
š--sh sound
ž--is like the 'su' sound in treasure

Some **consonants** that will throw you off:
c--is a ts sound
j--is y as in you
lj--is a difficult one for us! Try saying "lyoob"--the sides of your tongue will come up if you are doing it right.
Nj--like ny in canyon

7

Okay now for some **practice**:
lice (face)—did you say "L-I-S" like the dreadful insect?
Or did you say "lee-tsay", which would be the correct
way?
Let's try another one—stric (uncle)—did you say "strik"
or did you say "streets", the correct way?
Okay, last one--državljanin (citizen)--I'll just leave you
with that one...

Grammar

Okay, Bosnian is close to impossible to speak perfectly. Bosnian grammar is like English spelling—it makes absolutely no sense to an adult learner. So now you know what ESL students have to go through! Unlike other stereotypical Europeans, Bosnians are so pleased when a foreigner knows a few sentences in their language that they completely forgive any mistakes you might make! So just get out there and speak!

Here are a few rules of thumb that will make you sound like a pro! (Compared to other foreigners, anyway.)

1. Conjugations - Fun, fun, fun!

Normal verbs in the present tense:
There are three types of normal verbs, determined by their ending, sort of. The ending then changes according to person, like we add an "s" to most verbs in the third person, singular. Remember that they have the special word for *you* that is used for you-formal and you-plural so they don't have to say *y'all* or *yous-guys*. To make negations, just put "ne" in front of the verb. There is no need for helping verbs like "do".

-ati.1 verbs -		-iti verbs -	-ati.2 verbs
imate (to have) travel)		govoriti (to speak)	putovati (to
ja	imam	govorim	putujem
ti	imaš	govoriš	putuješ
on/a/o	ima	govori	putuje
mi	imamo	govorimo	putujemo
vi	imate	govorite	putujete
oni/e/a	imaju	govore	putuju

9

I know what you are thinking— how will I know which 'ati' verb it is? Well, that is what communication is all about— ask someone!!

Exceptions:

To Be	Biti	Agreement or confirmation
I am - I'm not	ja sam - nisam	jesam
You are - you aren't	ti si - nisi	jesi
he/she/it is - isn't	on/ona/ono je - nije	jeste
we are - aren't	mi smo - nismo	jesmo
you are - aren't	vi ste - niste	jeste
they are - aren't	oni/ona/one su- nisu	jesu

Htjeti (To want/wish/will)	Moći (to be able to)	Ići (to go)
hoću	mogu	idem
hoćeš	možeš	ideš
hoće	može	ide
hoćemo	možemo	idemo
hoćete	možete	idete
hoće	mogu	idu

GRAMMAR

And just to practice a bit, here are some useful verbs

To ask	pitati (ati.1)
To build	napraviti (iti)
To cheat	varati (ati.1)
To come	doći
To cry	plakati (irreg)
To dance	plesati (irreg)
To do	raditi, činiti (both iti)
To drink	piti (ati.2)
To drive	voziti (iti)
To eat	jesti (irreg)
To explain	objasniti (irreg)
To forgive	opraštati (ati.1)
To get	dobiti (irreg)
To give	dati (ati.2)
To go	ići
To help	pomoči (irreg)
To like	voliti / sviđa se / dopada se
To live	živiti (iti)
To look	gledati (ati.1)
To love	voliti (iti)
To make	praviti (iti)
To pay	platiti (ati.1)
To play	igrati (ati.1)
To practice	vježbati (ati.1)
To protect	štititi (iti)
To see	viditi (iti)
To sing	pjevati (ati.1)
To sleep	spavati (ati.1)
To speak	govoriti
To swim	plivati (ati.1)
To think	misliti (iti)
To try	probati (irreg)
To wake up	buditi (iti)

To walk	šetati (irreg)
To wash	oprati (ati.2)
To win	pobijediti (irreg)
To work	raditi (iti)
To worry	brinuti (ati.2)

The past...

Now this is pretty easy. Go back to the verb "biti" and add the past participle, depending on your gender and number.

How to make a past participle:

1. determine gender of person doing act
2. determine how many people did the act
3. take the root of the verb and add -o for males, -la for females, or -li for plural

Examples:

Ja sam govorila. On je imao. Mi smo putovali.
I (female) spoke. He had. We travelled.

More examples: **Biti**

I was	ja sam bila/bio
you were	ti si bila/bio
s/he was	ona je bila / on je bio
we were	mi smo bili
they were	oni su bili

To make it negative - use the negative form of "biti".

Caution - there are a few fancy things they do with word order, since their language does not depend on word order to determine what grammatical form the word takes. In English, "He gave it to me" or "To me he gave it" mean the same. We would not normally use the second sentence, but we understand it. We understand that it is not "I gave it to him" because "I" and "He" are subjects while "him" and "me" are objects. But usually, the subject comes first, then the verb, then the object. In other languages these forms are signified, not by placement, but by tags or changes in the word. So in those languages, of which Bosnian is one, sentence structure is more fluid, which English speakers can find rather confusing. So now you can't say that you haven't been warned. Shall we continue on?

Future Tense
This also shouldn't strain your brain. Go back to that strange looking verb "htjeti". You will never hear it like that, but everyday you will hear its forms, so get used to them. It means: will you? do you want? and it forms the future tense along with the infinitive...

I will be - won't be	ja ću biti - neću biti
you will be - " "	ti ćeš biti - nećeš biti
s/he will be	ona/on će biti - neće biti
we will be	mi ćemo biti - nećemo biti
they will be	oni će biti - neće biti

The Imperative - this is used for commands or suggestions.
In English, we just drop the object pronoun and raise our voice.
In Bosnian, they add a different ending to the verb stem.
 - **ati verbs** (1&2) add -aj, - ajmo, -ajte
example: slušati, listen: slušaj! slušajmo! slušjate!
 - **iti verbs** add -i, -imo, -ite
example: jesti, eat: jedi! jedimo! jedite! (and you *will* hear this one!)
To tell someone not to do something, just add "ne" to it:
 Don't cry - "Ne plačite" or "Ne plači"

Questions are a little more tricky...
Usually you put a "li" after the verb:
- Imate li kec? Do you have any aces? (Go Fish)
More formally, you start the sentence with "Da li":
- Da li je neko povrijeđen? Is anyone hurt?

Reflexive and Transitive Verbs

These are recognized by the "se" that follows the
infinitive. Truly reflexive verbs are things you do to
yourself, like wash yourself. The reflexive prounoun is
sebi or se. Transitive verbs are like passive tense.
"Sviđe mi se" is used for the verb "to like" but it really
means "It pleases me"; "Dopada mi se" means the same
thing.
It's a bit tricky to wrap your brain around this, but the
good thing is that usually you only see this in two forms,
it and *they.*

Examples:

Sviđa se: Sviđa **mi** se ova hrana - I like this food.
Sviđa **joj** se ovaj auto - She likes this car.
Dopa*da* se: Dopa*da* li **ti** se ovaj restoran? - Do you like
this restaurant?
Dopa*da* **im** se ova pjesma. They like this
song.
Those funny bold words you see in these sentences are
called object pronouns. But there are many kinds of
object pronouns in Bosnian.
Here are the ones you use with transitive verbs:

me - mi
you - ti
him - mu   us - nam
her - joj   you all - vam
them - im

GRAMMAR

Object Pronouns

with me	sa mnom
for me	za mene
with you	sa tobom
for you	za tebe
with her	sa njom
for her	za nju
with him	sa njim
for him	za njega
with us	sa nama
for us	za nas
with you all	sa vama
for you all	za vas
with them	sa njima
for them	za njih

It is important to have some grasp of this strange collection of words because they are used often and can occur in any part of a sentence, not just at the end where we would put them.

By now you might be getting the idea that there is something weird about Bosnian that does not exist in English, and you would be right! Now those of you who learned Latin in school might be familiar with words like dative, genitive, accusative, etc., but most of us are not, so we have no easy way of taking in these strange language structures. And frankly, why try? This is not a grammar book, this is a phrasebook! I'm only going into grammar insofar as it facilitates communication, but not to the point where it starts to impede it. Basically, the Bosnians will understand you if you don't get the adjective to match the noun, if you don't use any of those cases I just mentioned, and even if you don't conjugate verbs correctly. They may laugh at you but just think

that they are laughing *with* you, and start laughing so
you can catch up.

Conditional: If I were you....
In other languages, there are some high level verbal
stunts reserved for this part of speech but not in Bosnian,
thank goodness.
If... then...   =   ako... onda (except 3rd conditional)
(3rd cond.) If I were rich, I would buy a big house. Da
sam bogat, ja bih kupio/kupila veliku kuću.
(2nd cond.) If it rains tomorrow, then we will go to a
museum. Ako sutra bude padala kiša, onda ćemo ići u
muzej.
(1st cond.) If you are sick, then stay home. Ako si
bolestan, onda ostani kod kuće.

Verb prefixes
If you see these things added to a verb, don't get
worried! They are used to create a new, but somewhat
related verb. There doesn't seem to be any over-arching
function of these prefixes. Oh well.
po-
na-
iz -
za-

Bosnian-English

A

advokat	lawyer
aerodrom	airport
ako	if
ali	but
ambulanta, hitna	ambulance
apoteka	pharmacy
autostop	hitchhiking
avion	airplane
avionska pošta	airmail

B

baciti	throw, throw away
balavica	younger person who
musi	respect older ones
balkon, terasa	balcony
barikada	road block
bazen	swimming pool
benzin	gasoline
besmislica	nonsense
bez	without
bezobrazan	shameless, shameful
biber	pepper, black
biblioteka	library
bife	bar (pub, saloon)
bijelo	white
bilijar	pool, billiards
bilo gdje	anywhere
bilo kako	anyhow
bilo šta	anything
birati	choose
biser	pearl

biti	be
bitno je da	vital
bjesnilo	rabies
blagajna	ticket office
blato	mud
blijed	pale
blizanci	twins
blizu	near, close by
boca, flaša	bottle
Bog, Allah	God
bogat	rich
boja, farba	color
bojati se od...	afraid of
- bojim se...	- I'm afraid of..
- ne bojte se	- don't be afraid
bol	pain
bolan	painful
bolest leđa	backache
bolestan	ill, sick
bolji	better
bolnica	hospital
bolničarka	nurse
borba, bitka	fight
boriti se, borba	struggle
bračno stanje	marital status
brada	beard
brašno	flour
brat	brother
breskva	peach
brežuljak, brdo	hill
bridak	bitter
briga	care
brod, čamac	ship, boat
broj	number
brz	quick
brzina	speed

brzo	quickly
bubreg	kidney
bučan	noisy
budala, glupak	fool
budućnost	future
buka	noise

C

carina	customs, at borders
cijeli, potpun	whole
cijena	cost
cipele	shoes
crkva	church
crn	black
crna burza	black market
crven	red
Crveni Krst, Polumjesec	Red Cross, Crescent
cura	girlfriend
cvijet	flower

Ć, Č

čaj	tea
čak ako	even if...
čarape	socks
čaroban	charming
časna riječ?	honestly?
čekati	wait
čelo, ispred	front, in front
ćerka or kćerka	daughter
čestitam!	congratulations!
često	often
četka	brush (n.)
četvrt	quarter
čeznuti za domom	homesick
čir	ulcer
čist	clean (n.)

čistiti	clean (v.)
čitati	read
čizma	boot
čorba, supa	soup
čovjek	man
čudan	strange
čuvati se	take care!

D

da	yes
dalek	far
dalje	farther
dan	day
danas	today
dar, prilog	donation
dati, dopustiti	allow
dati, pokloniti	give
davno	ago (long ago)
debeo, debljina	fat
desno	right, not left
digitron	calculator
dijete	child
dim	smoke from fire
divan	lovely
divlji	wild, not tamed
djeca	children
djed	grandfather
djevojka, djevojčica	girl
dno	bottom
do, dok	until
doba, starost	age
dobar	good
dobiti	get
dobrodošao	welcome
dobrotvorne svrhe	charity
doći	arrive, come

dole, ispod	below
dolina	valley
dolje	down, as in not up
dolje, ispod	under
dom, kuča (house)	home
domaći	homemade
dopada mi se	like, as in I like...
doplata	extra charge
doručak	breakfast
dosada	boredom
dosadan	annoying
dosije	record, file
dosta	enough
došljaci	arrivals
doviđenja	good-bye
dozlogrdilo mi je	fed up with
dozvola	visa
dragocjen	valuable, precious
dragocjenosti	valuables
drevan	ancient
drug, drugica	companion
drugi, još jedan	other, another
državljanin	citizen
dug	debt
dugo	long, duration
dugovati	owe
duhan	tobacco
duša	soul
dvorac, zamak	castle

DŽ

džehenem, pakao	hell
džem	jam
dženet, raj	heaven

Đ

đaba, besplatan	free, as in no cost
đavo, vrag	devil

E

eno!	look, there!
eto!	there!
evo!	here you are! there!

F

fabrika, tvornica	factory
fakultet	college
foto-aparat	camera
frizer	hairdresser

G

gaćice	panties
gadan	nasty
gdje	where
gladan	hungry
glas	voice, vote, good news
glasan	loud
glava	head
glavobolja	headache
glavni	main
glavni grad	capital city
glavni štab	headquarters
gledati, pogledati	look, see
gležanj, zglob	ankle
gljiva	mushroom
gluh	deaf
glup	stupid
go	naked
godina	year

gomila	crowd
gore, naviše	up
gorivo	fuel
gospodin	sir, mister
gospođa	ma'am, madam
gospođica	miss, young woman
gost	guest
gostoprimstvo	hospitality
gotovina	cash
gotovo	nearly
govedina	beef
govoriti, pričati	talk
govoriti, tell=reći, talk=pričati	speak
govornik	speaker
grad	town
graditi, zidati	build
grah	bean
granica	border
grašak	peas
greška	fault, mistake
grijanje	heater
gripa	flu
grnčarija, keramika	pottery
grob	grave, in a cemetery
groblje	cemetery
grom	thunder
groznica	fever
grožđe	grapes
grub put	rough, rough road
gurati	push
guska	goose
guša	crops

H

haljina, odjeća	dress, clothes
hirurg	surgeon

hitan	urgent
hladan	cool
hljeb (or kruh in Croatian parts)	bread
hodati, šetati	walk
hrana	food
hvala	thank you

I

ići	go
igra, šala	game
igralište	playground
igrati se	play, as in let's
iko, svako, bilo ko	anyone
ili	or
imati	have
ime	name
inače	otherwise
iskusan	experienced
isprava	identification
ispričavati se, Izvinite	apologize, I apologize
istina	truth
istinit	true
isto	same
isto, takođe	also
istok	east
istraživati	explore
izaći	go out
izbjeglica	refugee
izbjeglički kamp	refugee camp
izbor, glasanje (voting)	election
izbor, izabran	choice, elect
izgledati	look, appear
izgubiti	lose
izključiti	switch off
izlaganje	exhibition
izlaz	exit

izlaz za nuždu	emergency exit
izlazite!	get out!
izlet pješke, pješačenje	hike
iznajmiti	rent
iznenađenje	amazing
izolovan	isolated
izraz	phrase
izvolite!	here you are! (giving something)
izvor	spring, water source

J

ja	I
jabuka	apple
jadan	poor, unfortunate
jagnje	lamb
jahaći konj	horseback riding
jaje	egg
jakna	jacket
javni	public
javni praznik	public holiday
jednom	once
jedno-smjerna ulica	one-way street
jednostavan	simple, not complicated
jeftin	cheap, as in price
jelen	deer
jelovnik	menu
jesen	autumn, fall
jesti	eat
jetra	liver
jezero	lake
jezik, govor	language
još jedan	extra, as in one more
juče	yesterday
jug	south

jutro	morning

K

kada	when
kajmak	sour cream
kako	how
kamen	stone
kamion	truck
kancelarija, ured	office
karta	ticket
karta u jednom pravcu	one way ticket
kasno, zakasnio/la	late
kašika	spoon
katanac, brava	lock
kazališni komad, predstava	play, as in theater
kazalište, pozorište	theater
keks	cookie
kikiriki	peanuts
kino	cinema, movies
kiselo	sour
kiša	rain
kišobran	umbrella
klanac	pass, mountain
klinci	kids, children
ključ	key
knjiga	book
knjižara	book shop
ko	who
kobasica	sausage
kod kuće, kod nas	at home, our place
kofer	suitcase
koji	which
koljeno	knee
komad	a piece
komadić	a little bit
komarac	mosquito

konačan	final
konačno! napokon	at last! eventually
konj	horse
konjska kola	horse and cart
korisno	helpful
koristan	useful
kosa	hair
kost	bone
košara, korpa	basket
košulja	shirt
kovati	beat (v.)
koza	goat
koža	leather, skin
krađa	theft
kraj	end
krastavac	cucumber
krasti	steal
kratak	short
krava	cow
krevet	bed
krhak	fragile
krijumčar	smuggler
križanje	cross, as in cross the street
krojač, šnajder	dressmaker
krompir	potato
kruška	pear
krv	blood
krvariti	bleed
kuća	house
kuhar/ica	cook (n.)
kuhati	cook (v.)
kuhinja	kitchen
kukuruz	corn
kula, toranj	tower
kupati se	bathe

27

kupatilo	bathroom
kupiti	buy
kurva	prostitute
kvalitet	quality

L

lagan	easy
lagano	light, as in not heavy
lagati	lie, as in tell a lie
lako	simple, easy
lavina, usov	avalanche
lažan, kriv	false
laži	lies
led	ice
leđa	back (body part)
leptir	butterfly
let	flight
lice	face
lijek	medication
lijen	lazy
lijep, divan	beautiful
lijevo	left, as in direction
likovna galerija	art gallery
logor	camping
lonac	kettle
lopta	ball, as in toy
loš	bad
lošiji	worse
loza	vine
lubenica	watermelon
lud	mad, crazy

LJ

ljepota, divota	beauty
ljeto	summer
ljubazno	kind, nice

ljubičast	purple
ljubomoran	jealous
ljudski	human
ljudski ispravno	human rights
ljut	mad, angry
ljut, papren	hot food
ljutit, bijesan	angry
ljutiti	annoy

M

mačka	cat
madrac	mattress
magarac	donkey
magla	fog
majka	mother
mali	small
mamurluk	hangover
manje, manji	less
manjina	minority
marka	stamp
maslac	butter
maslina	olive
mazga	mule
med	honey
medvjed	bear (animal)
međugradski razgovor	long distance call
meso	meat
mi	we
mijenjati novac	exchange money
mir, tišina	peace, quiet, silence
misao	thought
misliti	think
miš	mouse
mjesec	month, moon
mjesto	place (n.)
mješavina	mixture

mlad	young
mladić, dječak	youth, boy
mlijeko	milk
mlin	mill
mnogo, puno	many
moć	power, might
moćan	powerful
moguče	possible
mogućnost	possibility
moje, to je moje	mine, it's mine
mokar, vlažan	wet
molim	A polite word
meaning: please,	yes?, hello?
momak, dečko	boyfriend
morati	must
more	ocean
most	bridge
možda	maybe
mrav	ant
mraz	frost
mrtav	dead
mrziti	hate
mučenje	torture
mudrost	wisdom
munja	lightning
muški, muškarac	male, man
muž, suprug	husband

N

na	at, on
na dijelove	to take apart
na stranu	apart
na žalost	unfortunately
nacija, narod	nation
naći, zateći	find
nadimak	nickname

nadnica	wage, salary
nagrada	prize
najbolji	best
nakit	jewelry
napasti, napad	attack (v., n.)
napojnica	tip, restaurant
napolju	outdoors
narandža	orange (fruit)
narandžast	orange (color)
narod, ljudi	people
narodna igra, muzika	folk dancing, music
narodni	national
narodnost, nacionalnost	nationality
naručiti	order in a restaurant
nas	us
nasilje	violence
naš	our
natrag, iza	behind
nauka	science
naučnik	scientist
navijač	sports fan
navika, običaj	customs, in a culture
nazad	reverse
ne	no
nebo	sky
nećak	nephew
nećakinja	niece
nedostajete mi	miss, I miss you
nekako	somehow
neki	some
neko	someone
nekoliko	several, few
nema na čemu you're	don't mention it, welcome
nemoguć	impossible
nena, baka	grandmother

nenamješten	casual
neobičan	unusual
neplodan, jalov	barren
neprav	wrong
nepravedno	unfair
neprijatelj	enemy
neprijazan	unfriendly
nepušač	nonsmoker
nesporazum	misunderstanding
nesposobnost	disability
nesreća, nezgoda	accident
nesretan, jadan	unhappy
nestalo	run out of...
nestati	disappear
nešto	something
neudoban	uncomfortable
neuljudan, neprijatan	rude
nevrijme, oluja	storm
nezaposlen	unemployed
nezavisan	independent
nezavisnost	independence
nezdrav	unhealthy
nezgoda	trouble
nezgodan	inconvenient
nigdje	nowhere
nije valjda	oh no!
nijedan	none, neither
nikad	never
niko	nobody
nimalo	least
ništa	nothing
njegov, svoj	its
noć	night
nos	nose
nov	new
Nova godina	New Year

novčanik, tašna	wallet, purse
novinar	journalist
novine	newspapers
nož	knife
nula	zero

O

obala	shore
obaveza	obligation
obećanje	promise (n.)
obečavati	promise (v.)
običan	ordinary, usual
obično	usually
objed, obroci	meal/s
oblačan	cloudy
oboveza	require
očigledno	obvious
od	of, since
odgovor	answer (n.)
odgovoriti	answer (v.)
odlasci	departures
odletjeti u zrak	blow up, explode
odlično	excellent
odmah	immediately
odmoriti	rest, take it easy
odvratan	obnoxious
ogrjev, drvo za loženje	firewood
oko, oči	eye, eyes
okrenuti	turn around
okružje, kotar	district
olovka	pencil
omiljeni	favorite
on	he
ona	she
onesvijesti	passed out

oni, one, ona	they, those
opasan	dangerous
opasnost	danger, emergency
opoziv	cancellation
opustiti	relax
opuštajuče/a/i	relaxing
orah	walnut
ortak	business partner
osiguranje	insurance
osim	except
osjećati	feel, emotion
osjetljiv	alive
oslobođenje	liberation
osoba	person
ostatak	rest, take the rest
ostati	stay
oštar	sharp
otac	father
otići na put	go away
otok	island
otvoren	open, not closed
otvori	open (v.)
ovaj, ova, ono	this
ovca	sheep
ovdje	here
ovi, ove, ova	these
ozbiljan	serious, grave

P

pakao	hell
paket	package
pametan	smart
paprika	pepper, vegetable
para, novac	money
paradajz	tomato
partner	partner, sweetheart

pas	dog
pasoš	passport
pasti	fall down
pauza	break, as in tea or coffee
pazite!	look out!
pažljiv	careful
pčela	bee
pegla	iron, as in for clothes
peglati	iron (v.)
pekara	bakery
pepeljara	ashtray
pero	pen
peron, platforma	platform
piće	drink (n.)
pijaća voda	drinking water
pijan	drunk
pijesak	sand
pile	chicken
pilula	pill
pisati	write
pismo	letter
pitanje	question
pitati za, upitati	ask
piti	drink (v.)
pjesma	song
pješak	pedestrian
pjevati	sing
planina	mountain
plakat	poster
plakati	cry
platiti	pay
plav	blue
plaža	beach
plesanje, ples	dancing, dance
plin	gas, as in natural gas

plivati	swim
pljačka	robbery
pluća	lung
pobijediti	win
poboljšanje	improvement
početi	begin
početak	beginning, start
podići	get up
podne	midday
pogodan	convenient
pokazati	show (v.)
poklon, dar	present, gift
pokvareno	spoiled
pokvarenost	corruption
pola	half
pola *sedam* (halfway to 7:00)	half past six, 6:30
polako	slow
poljoprivreda	agriculture
poljubac	kiss
pomaknuti	move, change place
pomfrit	french fries
pomoć	help (n.)
pomoći, pomagati	aid (as in "to help")
pomoćni radnik	aid worker
ponoć	midnight
ponosan	proud
poplava	flood
popraviti	repair, mend, fix
porcija	helping of food
pored	next to
porod	birth
porodica	family
poruka	message
posao, rad	job, work
poseban	special
posjetilac	visitor

posjetiti	visit (v.)
poslastica	dessert
poslati	send
posljednji	last, final
poslije, nakon	after
poslije-podne	afternoon
poslovno preduzeće	business enterprise
pospan	sleepy
postati	become
postići, pobijediti	beat (win)
posuditi, uzajmiti	borrow
poštansko sanduče	mail box
pošten	honest
pošto, puno	much (how much, a lot)
potok	stream
potpis	signature
potpisati se	sign, to write your name
potreban	necessary
potreba	need (n.)
potres	earthquake
povratak	return
povratna karta	return ticket
povrće	vegetables
povreda	injury
povremeno	occasionally
područje	area
pozajmiti	lend
poziv	invitation
pozvati	invite
požar!!	fire!!
požuri!	hurry up!
praonica, rublja, veša	laundry
prase, svinja	pig
prati (se)	wash

pravac, smijer	route, direction
pravda	fair, just, justice
praviti, izraditi, raditi	make
praznik, odmor	holiday
predgrađe	suburb
prednost	priority, preference
predomislila/-o sam se	mind, I changed my mind
predstaviti	introduce
preduzeće	business
pregovarač	negotiator
prehladiti se	catch cold
prekasno	too late
prekid, lom, slomjen	break (v.)
preko	via
preko, nad	over
prekoputa	opposite, across from
prelom	fracture
prema	towards
premda	although
preporučiti	recommend
prepun	crowded
presijedati	change, as in trains, busses, etc
pretežak	overweight
previše	too many
prevodilac	interpreter, translator
prevoditi	interpret, translate
prezime	last name
prijatan, ljubazan	nice
prijatan, ugodan	pleasant, enjoyable
prijatelj, -ica	friend
prije	before
prilika	opportunity
primirje	truce, cease-fire
primjer	example

priroda	countryside
prirodan	natural
pristanak, sporazum	agreement
pristao	handsome
pritisak	pressure
pritužba	complaint
priznanje	confession
prljavo	dirty
probati	try
proći	pass by someone
prodati	sell
prodavati, za prodaju	sale, for sale
prohodan	passable road
proljeće	spring, season
proljev	diarrhea
promatrač	observer
promjena	change, as in not the same
promjena pravca	U-turn
promjena novca	change, as in money exchange
prošli	last, past (last year)
prošlost	past, not future
protivzakonito	against the law
prozor	window
prtljaga	luggage
prvi	first
pšenica	wheat
ptica	bird
pun	full
pun mjesec	full moon
puno, mnogo	lot, a lot
puran, ćuran	turkey
pušiti	smoke cigarettes
puška	rifle
put, cesta	road

putnik	passenger, traveller
putovanje	journey
putovati	travel (v.)

R

račun, list, cedulja	check, bill, something to pay
računovođa	accountant
radije	preferably
radije bih...../ ne bih	rather, I'd rather../ not
radno vrijeme	opening time
radostan	glad
raj, dženet	heaven
rak	crab, cancer
rano	early
rasa	race, ethnicity
raseljeno lice	displaced person, DP
raskrsnica	crossroads, intersection
raspust	vacation
rastavaljen/a	divorced
rat	war
ratni zločini	war crimes
ravan	plain, flat land, level
razdvojeno	separate
razgledanje	sightseeing
razglednica	postcard
razgovor	conversation
različiti	different
razlog	reason (n.)
razonoda	pastime
razumjeti	understand
recept	prescription
reći	say, tell
red	queue
repa	beet

riba	fish
ribolov	fishing
riječnik	dictionary
riječnik fraza	phrase book
rijedak	rare, hard to find
rijeka	river
rijetko	seldom
rikverc, unazad	back up
rizično	risky
riža	rice
robna kuća	department store
roditelji	parents
roditi	give birth
rodni list	birth certificate
rođak, rodica	cousin
rođen	born
rođendan	birthday
ručak	lunch
rudnik	mine, coal
rudnik ugljena	coal mine
ruka	arm
rukovodilac	leader
ruksak	backpack
rupa, jama	hole
ruševine	ruins
ružan	ugly

S	
sa	with
sada	now
sam	alone
samac	single, not married
samo	only
san	dream
saobračaj	traffic
saobraćajna gužva	traffic jam

sapun	soap
sasvim	quite
sasvim slučajno	chance
sastanak	meeting
sat	clock, hour
savršen	perfect
sebe, se	itself
sedmica	week
seliti	move, change homes
seljak-seljaci (impolite term)	peasant, peasants
selo	village
semafor	traffic light
senf	mustard
sestra	sister
SIDA	AIDS
siguran	safe, certain
sigurnost	safety
sijati sjeme	plant seeds
sijeno	hay
silovanje	rape
sin	son
sir	cheese
sirće	vinegar
siroče	orphan
siromašan	poor, not rich
sirov	raw
sitno, sitniš	change, as in small money
sjediti	sit
sjeme, klica	seed
sjena	shadow
sjever	north
skok, skočiti	jump
skela	ferry
skoro	almost
skreni lijevo/desno	turn left/right

skroman	plain, not fancy
skroz	all, complete, the
whole thing skup	expensive
slab	weak
sladoled	ice cream
slan	salty
slani keks	crackers
slatka	sweet
slatkoća	sweetness
sličan	alike, similar
slijep	blind (can't see)
slijepa ulica	dead end
slika	painting
slika, crtež	picture
slika, snimak (shot)	photograph
sljedeći	next
sloboda	freedom
slobodan	free, as in liberty
slomiti	break down, as in car problems
slomljeno srce	broken heart
slušati	listen
služba	service
službenik	official (n.)
smanjiti	lower
smeće	rubbish, junk
smeđ	brown
smijati se	laugh
smiješiti se	smile
smisao za humor	sense of humor
smrdi	smelly
smrt	death
snažan	strong
snijeg	snow
soba	room
sol	salt

43

spasiti	rescue
spavati	sleep
spolna bolest	venereal disease
sposobnost, vještina	ability
spreman	ready
sprovod, đenaza	funeral
srce	heart
srčani napad	heart attack
srebro	silver
sreća	lucky
srednje-veličine	medium-sized
sresti	meet
sretan, veseo	lucky, happy
sretno!	good luck!
srušen	ruined
stablo	tree
stambeni blok	apartment block
stambeni projekt	housing project
stan	apartment
stanica	station
star	old
stari grad	old town
staromodan	old-fashioned
staza	path
stidan	shy
stiglo	yet
stijena	rock
stjenica, kukac	bug
sto	table
sto, stotina	hundred
stolica	chair
stran, tuđi	foreign
stranac	stranger, foreigner
stranka	party, political
strašan, grozan	terrible
straža	wristwatch

stručnjak	expert
struja	power, energy
stvar, predmet (subject)	thing
stvaran, pravi	real
stvarno, zaista	really
sudija	judge
suh	dry
sunce	sun
sunčan	sunny
sunčane naočale	sunglasses
suosječajnost	sympathy
suprotan	opposite
susjed, komšija	neighbor
susjedstvo, komšiluk	neighborhood
sutra	tomorrow
suviše, previše	too many/much
svakako	certainly
svaki	every
svako	everyone
sve, sav, cijeli (whole)	all, everything
svejedno mi je	I don't mind
svidjeti se	please, as in I like it
svijeća	candle
svijet	world
svijetlo	light, as in lamp and color
svinjetina	pork
svjež	fresh
svrab	itch
svuda	everywhere

Š

šah	chess
šala	joke
šaliti	kidding
šaljiv	funny

šator	tent
šećer	sugar
šibice	matches
širok	wide
škola	school
škrt	stingy
šlag	whipped cream
šok	shock, surprise
šou	show (n.)
špijun	spy
špilja	cave
štakor	rat
štala, štagalj	barn
šteta	it's a pity
štititi	protect
što, šta	what
šuma	wood and woods

T

tačno!	exactly!
tajna	secret
tako	so
talac	hostage
taman	dark
tamo, ondje	there
tanak	thin
teletina	veal
težak, mučan	difficult, hard
težak, teško/a	heavy
težina	weight
tijesan	tight
tišina	silence
tjestenina	pasta
toplo	warm
torba, kesa	bag
torta, kolač	cake

trajan	last, enduring
trava	grass
trave	herbs
tražiti	look for
trčati	run
trebati	need, verb
trenutak	moment
trgovina	market
trk!	run!
trka	race, competition
trudna	pregnant
tuš	shower
tužan	sad
tvoj (fam), vaš (pl)	your, yours

U

u	in
u kvaru je, ne radi	out of order
u pomoć!	help!!!
u pravu, tačan	right, as in not wrong
u redu	OK
u sredini	middle
ubica	killer
ubijen/a /-ni	murdered (m., f., pl.)
ubiti	kill
učenik	student
učitelj	teacher
učiti, podučavati	teach
učiti	learn
učtiv	polite
udaja, ženidba	marriage (f., m.)
udaljeno	remote
udar	shock, electrical
udata, oženjen	married (f., m.)
udoban	comfortable
udovica	widow

ugao, na uglu	corner, on the corner
ugriz, ubod	bite (n.)
uho	ear
ujed/ugriz insekta	insect bite
uključeno	included
uključiti	switch on
ukrasti nekoga, radi novca	kidnap
ukupno	total
ukusan	tasty, delicious
ulazak, pristup	entrance
ulica	street
ulje, nafta (diesel)	oil
umjesto	instead
umjetnik	artist
umoran	tired
umorstvo, ubistvo	assassination
umrijeti, preminuti	die
unutar	into
unutra	inside
upala slijepog crijeva	appendicitis
upotrijebiti	use
upravitelj	administrator
uredan	neat
useljenje	immigration
uskoro	soon
usput rečeno	by the way...
ustaj!	get up! (get out of bed)
uvijek	always
uvreda	insult (n.)
uz	by
uzajamno, jedan drugog	each other
uzak	narrow
uzeti	take

V

van, napolje	out
vani	outside
vatra	fire
vatreno oružje	firearms
važan	important
već	already
većina	majority
veče	evening
večera	dinner, supper
večeras	tonight
veličina	size
velik	large
ventilator	fan
veoma, vrlo	very
vid	eyesight
vidik, pogled	view
vidjeti	see
vidljivost	visability
vijest	news
viljuška	fork
visina	height
visok	tall
više	more
više volite	prefer
vitak	slim
vjenčanje	wedding
vjerojatno	probably
vjerovati	believe
vještački udo	artificial limb
vještina	ability
vjetar, dah	wind, as in blows
vjetrovit	windy
vježbati	practice
vlada, uprava	government
vlasnik	owner

voće	fruit
voćni sok	fruit juice
voćnjak	orchard
voda	water
vodič	guide
vodič knjiga	guidebook
vodimo ljubav	make love
voditi rat	wage war
vodopad	waterfall
vojnik	soldier
voljeti	love
voz, vlak	train
vozač	driver
vozačka dozvola	driver's license
voziti	drive
vrh	top
vrijednost	value (n.)
vrijeme	time, weather
vrsta, sorta	kind, sort, variety
vrt, bašta	garden
vruć	hot (temperature)
vruća voda	hot water
vrućina	heat
vući	pull
vuk	wolf
vuna	wool

Z

zabava	party
zaboraviti	forget
zabraniti	forbid
zabrinut	worried
začinjen, ljut	spicy
zagađen	polluted
zajedno	together
zaključano je	locked

zakon	law
zalazak sunca	sunset
zalogaj	snack
zamijeniti	exchange
zanat	handicraft
zanimljiv	interesting
zaostao	backwards
zapad	west
zapamtiti	remember
zaposlen, zauzet	busy
zaraza	infection
zarazan	epidemic
zaroniti!	duck! as in get down
zastava	flag
zastoj saobraćaja	traffic jam
zaštita	protection
zašto	why
zatvor	prison
zatvoren	closed, as in not open
zatvoriti	shut
završiti	finish
zbrka, nered	mess
zdenac, izvor	well, water
zdrav	healthy
zdravlje	health
zdravo!	hello!
zec	rabbit
zelen	green
zemlja, domovina	country
zemlja	ground, earth
zemljoradnik	farmer
zgrada	building
zima	winter
zlato	gold
zločin	crime
zmija	snake

znak	sign, stop sign
znati	know
zoološki vrt	zoo
zora, svanuće, sabah	dawn, sunrise
zrak, vazduh	air
zub	tooth
zubar	dentist
zubi	teeth
zubobolja	toothache
zvati	call (verb)
zvijezda	star

Ž

žaba	frog
žao	sorry
žedan	thirsty
željeti	wish
željeznica	railway
željeznička stanica	train station
žena	women
žena, supruga	wife
ženski	female
žetva, berba	harvest
židov, jevrej	Jewish
žilav	tough
živahan, živ	lively person, place
živjeti	live
život	life
životinja	animal
žurba	hurry
žuto	yellow

English-Bosnian

A

ability	sposobnost, vještina
about (I'm talking about...)	kod, o, oko, za
academic	akademski
accident	nesreća, nezgoda
accountant	računovođa
adapter (electrical thing)	radio i TV adapter
address (where someone lives)	adresa
administrator	upravitelj, administrator
afraid of	bojati se od...
- I'm afraid of..	bojim se...
- don't be afraid	ne bojte se
after	nakon, poslije
afternoon	poslije-podne
- yesterday afternoon	juče popodne
age	doba, starost
ago (long ago)	davno
ago (one year ago)	prije godinu dana
agreement	pristanak, sporazum
agriculture	poljoprivreda
aid worker	pomoćni radnik
aid (as in "to help")	pomoći, pomagati
AIDS	SIDA
air	zrak, vazduh
airmail	avionska pošta
airplane	avion
airport	aerodrom
alcohol	alkohol
alike	sličan
alive	osjetljiv
all	sve, sav, cijeli
- that's all!	To je sve!
allergic	alergičan

allergy	alergija
allow	dati, dopustiti
almost	skoro
alone	sam
already	već
- I've already eaten	Ja sam već jela, Već sam jela
also	isto, takođe
although	premda
always	uvijek
amazing	iznenađenje
ambulance	ambulanta, hitna
American	(f) amerikanka, (m) amerikanac
amputation	amputacija
ancient	drevan
and	i, a, pa
anemia	anemija
angry	ljutit, bijesan
animal	životinja
ankle	gležanj, zglob
annoy	ljutiti
annoying	dosadan
another	drugi, još jedan
answer (verb)	odgovoriti
answer (noun)	odgovor
ant	mrav
anyhow	bilo kako
anyone	iko, svako, bilo ko
anything	bilo šta
anywhere	bilo gdje
apart	na stranu, posebnu
- to take apart	na dijelove
apartment	stan
apartment block	stambeni blok
apologize, I apologize	ispričavati se, Izvinite

appendicitis	upala slijepog crijeva
apple	jabuka
architect	arhitekt
architecture	arhitektura
area	područje
arm	ruka
arrest (police thing)	zatvor
arrivals	došljaci
arrive	doći
art gallery	likovna galerija
artificial limb	vještački udo
artist	umjetnik
ashtray	pepeljara
ask	pitati za, upitati
assassination	umorstvo, ubistvo
asthmatic	asmatičar
at	na, u
at home, our place	kod kuće, kod nas
at last!	konačno! napokon
at least	najmanje
attack (v., n.)	napasti, napad
autumn	jesen
avalanche	lavina
axe	sjekira

B

back (body part)	leđa
back up	rikverc, unazad
backache	bolest leđa
backpack	ruksak
backwards	zaostao
bad	loš
bag	torba, kesa
bakery	pekara
balcony	balkon, terasa
bank	banka

ball, as in toy	lopta
ball, as in dance	ples
bar (pub, saloon)	bife, bar
barn	štala, štagalj
barren	neplodan, jalov
basement	temelj, podrum
basket	košara, korpa
bathe	kupati se
bathroom	WC, kupatilo
be	biti
beach	plaža
bean	grah
bear (animal)	medvjed
bear (nude)	gol
bear (tolerate)	ustrajati
bear (carry)	nositi
beard	brada
beat (hit)	kovati
beat (win)	pobijediti
- I won!	ja sam pobijed-io/la!
beautiful	lijep, divan
beauty	ljepota, divota
become	postati
bed	krevet
bee	pčela
beef	govedina
beet	repa
before	prije
begin	početi
beginning	početak
behind	natrag, iza
believe	vjerovati
below	dole, ispod
belt	pojas, remen
bend	krivina, okuka
best	najbolji

better	bolji
- I feel better	Ja se osjećam bolje
bicycle	biciklo
big	velik, krupan
bill, as in somthing to pay	račun, list, cedulja
bird	ptica
birth	porod
birth certificate	rodni list
birth control	sprečavanje trudnoće
birthday	rođendan
- happy birthday!	sretan rođendan!
bit, a bit	komadić
bite (n.)	ugriz, ubod
bite (v.)	zagristi, ugristi
bitter	bridak
black	crn
black market	crna burza
blanket	deka, čebe
bleed	krvariti
blind (can't see)	slijep
blizzard	sniježna mečava
block (noun)	klada, blok
block (verb)	blokirati
blood	krv
blow, as in wind	puhati
blow up, explode	odletjeti u zrak, eksplodirati
blow your nose!	oseknuti se!
blue	plav
board, made of wood	daska
boat	brod, čamac
body	tijelo, trup
bomb	bomba
bone	kost
book	knjiga
bookstore	knjižara

boot	čizma
border	granica
border crossing	granični prelaz
boredom	dosada
born	rođen
- I was born in ...	Ja sam rođen u...
borrow	posuditi, uzajmiti
bother	gnjaviti se
- I don't want to bother you	Ja ne želim vas gnjaviti.
- It's no bother!	To nije gnjavaža!
bottle	boca, flaša
bottom	dno
box	kutija
boy	mladić, dječak
boyfriend	momak, dečko
bracelet	narukvica
brain	mozak, razum
brainless	bez pameti
brake, on a car	kočnica
brave	hrabar, srčan
bread	hljeb (or kruh in Croatian parts)
break, as in whoops!	prekid, lom, slomljen
break, as in tea or coffee	pauza
break down, as in car problems	slomiti
breakfast	doručak
brick	opeka
bridge	most
bring	donijeti, dati
broken heart	slomljeno srce
brother	brat
brown	smeđ
brush (noun)	četka
bucket	vedro, čabar
bug	stjenica, kukac

build	graditi, zidati
building	zgrada
bull	bik
bullet	kugla, tane
burn	opekotina
bus	autobus
- you missed the bus	- propustili ste autobus
bus station	autobuska stanica
business	biznis, preduzeće
business enterprise	poslovno preduzeće
business person	poslovan čovjek
busy	zaposlen, zauzet
but	ali
butter	maslac
butterfly	leptir
buy	kupiti
by	uz
by the way...	usput rečeno

C

cake	torta, kolač
calculator	digitron
call (noun)	poziv
call (verb)	zvati
camera	foto-aparat, kamera
camera equipment	oprema za kameru
camping	logor
can, as in able	moći
can, as in tin	konzerva
can opener	otvarač konzervi
cancellation	opoziv
- there has been a cancellation	- bio je opoziv
cancer	rak
candle	svijeća
candy	bombon

capital city	glavni grad
car	auto
care	briga
- take care! - be careful!	pazite!
- take care of...	brinuti se za...
I don't care about it.	svejedno mi je
career	karijera
careful	pažljiv
caress	milovanje
carpenter	tesar
carpet	ćilim
cash	gotovina, keš
castle	dvorac, zamak
casual	nenamješten
cat	mačka
catch	ulov, hvatanje
- catch cold	prehladiti se
cattle	stoka, marva
cause	povod, razlog
cave	špilja
ceasefire	primirje
cellar	podrum
cemetery	groblje
century	vijek, stoljeće
certain	siguran
- are you certain?	jeste li sigurni?
- I'm absolutely certain!	ja sam potpuno siguran!
certainly	svakako
chain	lanac
chair	stolica
chance	sasvim slučajno
change, as in not the same	promjena
change, as in money exchange	promjena novca
change, as in small money	sitno, sitniš
change, as in trains, buses, etc	presijedati

charge, as in leader	briga
- who's in charge?	ko se brine? ko je zadužen
charity	dobrotvorne svrhe
charming	čaroban
chase	potjera
cheap, as in price	jeftin
cheap, as in low quality	bez kvaliteta
cheat	prevariti
check, as in bill	račun
check, as in look	provjeriti
cheese	sir
chess	šah
chicken	pile
child	dijete
children	djeca
choice	izbor, izabran
choose	birati
church	crkva
cinema	kino
citizen	državljanin
civil rights	civilna/građanska prava
civil war	građanski rat
civilian	civilni
clean (n.)	čist
clean (v.)	čistiti
clock	sat
close, as in near	blizu
closed, as in not open	zatvoren
cloudy	oblačan
coal mine	rudnik ugljena
coat	kaput, jakna
coffee	kafa
- with milk and sugar	sa mlijekom i sečerom

- without sugar	bez sečer
coins	sitniš
cold	hladno, zima
college	fakultet
color	boja, farba
comb	češalj
come	doći
- come in!	slobodno! uđite
- come here!	dođite ovamo!
- come again!	dođite ponovo
- come back!	vratite se!
- I'll come back later	vratit ću se kasnije
- she comes from Brčko	ona je iz Brčkog (sic)
- where do you come from?	odakle ste vi?
comfortable	udoban
companion	drug, drugarica
complaint	pritužba
condom	prezervativ
confess	priznati
confession	priznanje
congratulations!	čestitam!
consultant	savjetnik
convenient	pogodan
conversation	razgovor
convoy	konvoj, pratnja
cook (v.)	kuhati
cook (n.)	kuhar/ kuharica
cookie	keks
cool	hladan
copy	kopija
corn	kukuruz
corner, on the corner	ugao, na uglu
corruption	korupcija, pokvarenost
cost	cijena
cough	kašalj

count	brojati
country	zemlja, domovina
countryside	priroda
couple	par
couple, few, some	nekoliko
cousin	rođak, rodica, rođaka
cow	krava
crab	rak
crackers	slani keks
cramp, muscle	grč
cream, whipped cream	šlag
crime	zločin
criminal	zločinački
crisis	kriza
crops	guša
cross, as in cross the street	križanje
crossroads	raskrsnica
crow	vrana
crowd	gomila
crowded	prepun
cruel	grozan
cry	plakati
- don't cry!	ne plačite!
cucumber	krastavac
cup	čaša, šalica
cupboard	orman
currency	cirkulacija, valuta
customs, at borders	carina
customs, in a culture	navika, običaj
cut, as in ouch	posjeći
- cut off a piece	odsjeći komad
- cut off, phone experience	prekinuto je

D

dairy	mljekara
dam	brana, nasip

dancing, dance	plesanje, ples
danger	opasnost
dangerous	opasan
dark	taman
date of...	datum
- arrival	dolaska
- birth	poroda
- departure	odlaska
daughter	ćerka, kćerka
dawn	zora, svanuće, sabah
day	dan
dead	mrtav
dead end	slijepa ulica
deaf	gluh
death	smrt
debt	dug
decade	decenija
decide	odlučiti
deep	dubok
- how deep is it?	koliko je duboko to?
deer	jelen
defeat	poraziti
defend	braniti, štititi
delay	odgađanje
democracy	demokracija
democratic	demokratski
demonstration	demonstracija
dentist	zubar
department store	robna kuća
departures	odlasci
deprive	lišiti
desk	pult, šalter
dessert	poslastica
destroy	razoriti, uništiti
devil	đavo, vrag
diabetic	dijabetičar

diagnosis	dijagnoza
diarrhea	proljev
dictator	diktator
dictatorship	diktatura
dictionary	riječnik
die	umrijeti, preminuti
diesel	dizel
diet	dijeta
different	različito
difficult	težak, mučan
dig	kopati
dinner, supper	večera
direct (adj)	direktan
direction	pravac
dirty	prljavo
disability	nesposobnost
disappear	nestati
disappointed	razočaran
disaster	katastrofa
discussion	rasprava
disgusting	odvratan
disease	bolest
displaced person, DP	raseljeno lice
dispute	prepirka
distance	daljina
distant	dalek
district	okružje, kotar
disturb, bother	uznemiravati
divorced	rastavljen/a
do	raditi (work), činiti (perform)
dog	pas
doll	lutka
donkey	magarac
door	vrata
double bed, room	dupli krevet, sobe

doubt	sumnjati
- I doubt it	sumnjam
dough	tijesto
down, as in not up	dolje
drain, in a sink	prokop
draw, as in art	izvući, povući
dream	san
dress	odjeća, haljina
dressmaker	krojač, šnajder
drink (v.)	piti
drink (n.)	piće
- is the water drinkable?	je li voda za piće?
drinking water	pijaća voda
drive	voziti
driver	vozač
driver's license	vozačka dozvola
dry	suh, suv
drug	droga
drum	bubanj, bubnjeve
drunk	pijan
duck, as in quack	patka
duck! as in get down	zaroniti!
during	za vrijeme

E

each	svaki
each other	uzajamno, jedan drugog
ear	uho
early	rano
earth	zemlja
earthquake	potres
east	istok
easy	lagan, lako
eat	jesti
egg	jaje

either...or	ili...ili
elbow	lakat
elect	izabran
election	izbor, glasanje (voting)
electricity	električna struja
elevator	dizalica
else - something else	nešto drugo
- somewhere else	negdje drugdje
- what else?	šta još?
- nothing else, no more	ništa drugo, nema više
embarrassing	nezgodan
emergency	opasnost
- this is an emergency!	ovo je hitan slučaj!
emergency exit	izlaz za nuždu
empty	prazan
end	kraj
enemy	neprijatelj
engine	stroj
engineer	inženjer
enjoyable	prijatan
enormous	ogroman
enough	dosta
enter	unijeti, ući
entrance	ulazak, pristup
envelope	koverta
epidemic	zarazan
epileptic	padavičar
equipment	oprema, pribor
eraser	brisač, gumica
escape (n., v.)	bjeg, bježati
ethnic cleansing	etničko čiščenje
Europe	Evropa
even if...	čak ako
evening	veče

eventually	konačno
ever	ikad (see adv. conv. chapter)
every	svaki
everyone	svako
everything	sve
everywhere	svuda
exactly!	tačno!
exam	ispit
example	primjer
excellent	odlično
except	osim
exchange	zamijeniti
exchange money	mijenjati novac
exciting	uzbudljiv
excluded	isključen
excuse me	oprostite, izvinite
exhausted	premoren
exhibition	izlaganje
exile	izgon
exit	izlaz
expel	izbaciti
expensive	skup
experience	doživljaj
experienced	iskusan
expert	stručnjak
explain	objasniti
explode	eksplodirati
explore	istraživati
express, as in fast train, mail	ekspres
express, as in demonstrate	hitan
extra, as in one more	još jedan, ekstra
extra charge	doplata
extra special	poseban
eye, eyes	oko, oči
eyesight	vid

F

face	lice
factory	tvornica, fabrika
failure	neuspjeh
fair, just	pošteno, pravda
fall down	pasti
fall, autumn	jesen
false	lažan, kriv
family	porodica
fan	ventilator
fan of sports	navijač
far	dalek
farm	farma
farmer	zemljoradnik
farther	dalje
fast, quick	brz
fast, not eating	post, postiti
fat	debeo, debljina
father	otac
fault, mistake	greška
favorite	omiljeni
fear	strah
fed up with	dozlogrdilo mi je
feel (emotion)	osjećati
feel (touch)	pipati
female	ženski
fence	plot ograda
ferry	skela
feud	svađa, zavada
fever	groznica
few	nekoliko
field	polje, igralište
fight	borba, bitka
fighter	borac
file	fascikl

fill	napuniti
film	film
final	konačan, finalan
find	naći, zateći
finger	prst
finish	završiti
fire	vatra
fire!!	požar!!
firewood	ogrjev, drvo za loženje
first	prvi
fish	riba
fishing	ribolov
fix	popraviti
- can you fix it?	možete li popraviti?
flag	zastava
flash of light	bljesak, sjaj
flashlight	lagano svjetlo, baterija
flat	ravan
flea	buha
flee	bježati
flight	let
flood	poplava
floor	patos, pod
flour	brašno
flower	cvijet (world = svijet)
flu	gripa
fly (n.)	muha
fly (v.)	letjeti
fog	magla
folk dancing, music	narodna igra, muzika
food	hrana
fool	budala, glupak
foot	noga
forbid	zabraniti

foreign	stran, tuđi
foreigner	stranac
forest	šuma
forget	zaboraviti
fork	viljuška
forwards	naprijed
four wheel drive	pogon na četiri točka
fracture	prelom
fragile	krhak
free, as in liberty	slobodan
free, as in no cost	džaba, besplatan
freedom	sloboda
freeze	smrznuti se
french fries	pomfrit
fresh	svjež
fridge	frižider
friend	prijatelj, -ica (drug - comrade)
frog	žaba
front, in front	čelo, ispred
frost	mraz
fruit	voće
fruit juice	voćni sok
fuel	gorivo
full	pun
- I'm full	sit/a sam
full moon	pun mjesec
funeral	sprovod, dženaza
funny	šaljiv
future	budućnost

G

game, joke	igra, šala
garden	vrt, bašta
gas	plin
gasoline	benzin

germs	klice
get	dobiti
get up	podići
get up! (get out of bed)	ustaj!
gift	poklon, dar
girl	djevojka, djevojčica
girlfriend	cura
give birth	roditi
give	dati, pokloniti
glad	radostan
glass, material	staklo
glass for drinking	čaša
glasses	naočare
go	ići
- go away	otići na put
- go away!	gubi se!
- go out	izaći
- let's go!	hajdemo!
goat	koza
God	Bog, Allah
gold	zlato
good	dobar
good-bye	doviđenja
goose	guska
gossip	naklapanje, treč
government	vlada, uprava
grandchild	unuće, unuk
grandchildren	unuci, unućad
grandfather	djed, đedo
grandmother	nena, baka, nana
grapes	grožđe
grass	trava
grateful	zahvalan, ugodan
grave, in a cemetery	grob
grave, serious	ozbiljan
green	zelen

grenade	granata
grind	mrviti, drobiti
ground, below us	zemlja
ground, small pieces	mljeven/a/o
grow	porasti
- grow crops	zadovoljstvo
- grow up	prirasti
guest	goste
guide	vodič
guidebook	vodič knjige
guilty	kriv
gun	pištolj, revolver
guy	čovjek

H

hair	kosa
hairbrush	četka za kosu
hairdresser	frizer
hairdryer	suha kosa
half	pola
- half past six	pola *sedam* (halfway to 7:00)
hammer	čekić, malj
hand	ruka, šaka
handbag	ručna torba
handicraft	zanat
handsome	pristao
handy	priručan
hangover	mamurluk
happen	dogoditi se
- how did it happen?	kako se to dogodilo?
- what happened here?	šta se dogodilo ovdje?
happy	sretan (lucky), veseo
- I'm happy with it	sviđa mi se
harbor	luka
hard	tvrd

hard (difficult)	težak
harm, noun	šteta
harvest	žetva, berba
hat	šešir
hate	mrziti
have	imati
have to, must	morati
hay	sijeno
hay fever	peludna groznica
haystack	stog sijena
he	on
head	glava
headache	glavobolja
headquarters	glavni štab
health	zdravlje
healthy	zdrav
hear	čuti
- can you hear me?	čujete li me?
- I can't hear you!	ne čujem vas!
- I've heard about it.	čuo sam za to.
heart	srce
heart attack	srčani napad, infarkt
heat	vrućina
heater	grijanje, grijalica (room)
heaven	raj, dženet
heavy	težak, teško/a
height	visina
hell	dženem/pakao
hello!	zdravo!
help (n.)	pomoć
help (v.)	pomoći
help!!!	u pomoć!
helpful	korisno, koristan
helping of food	porcija

her	
- with her	s njom
- for her	za nju
- her name	njeno ime
- hers	njen
- that's hers	to je njeno
- herself	ona lično
herbs	trave
here	ovdje
- here you are! (giving smth.)	izvolite!
- here she comes	evo ga
hide, as in hide and seek	sakriti
high	visok, snažan, jak
hike	izlet pješke, pješačenje
hill	brežuljak, brdo
him	
- with him	s njim
- for him	za njega
- him name	njeno ime
- his	njegov
- that's his	to je njegovo
- himself	on lično
hitchhiking	autostop
hold	držati
hole	rupa, jama
holiday	praznik, odmor
home	dom, kuća (house)
homemade	domaći
homesick	čeznuti za domom
honest	pošten
honestly?	časna riječ?
honey	med
horse	konj
- and cart	konjska kola
- riding	jahaći konj

hospital	bolnica
hospitality	gostoprimstvo
hostage	talac
hostel	prenoćiste
hot (temperature)	vruć
hot food	ljut, papren
hot water	vruća voda
hour	čas, sat
house	kuća
housing project	stambeni projekt
how	kako
human	ljudski
human rights	ljudska prava
humid	vlažan
humor, sense of	smisao za humor
hundred	sto, stotina
hungry	gladan
hurry	žurba
- hurry up!	požuri!
hurt, feel	boli
hurt someone	ozlijediti
husband	muž, suprug

I

I	ja
ice	led
ice cream	sladoled
idea	ideja, misao (thought)
identification	isprava
if	ako
ill	bolestan
immediately	odmah
immigration	useljenje
important	važan
impossible	nemoguć
improvement	poboljšanje

in	u
included	uključeno
inconvenient	nezgodan
incredible	nevjerovatan
independence	nezavisnost
independent	nezavisan
infection	infekcija, zaraza
information	informacije
injury	povreda
in-laws of husband, of wife	porodica moje žene/mog muža
innocent (means virgin!)	nevin
- not guilty	nedužan
insane	lud
insect	insekt
insect bite	ujed/ugriz insekta,
inside	unutra
instead	umjesto
insult (n.)	uvreda
insurance	osiguranje
intelligent	inteligentan
interesting	zanimljiv, interesantan
interpret	prevoditi
interpreter	prevodilac
intersection	raskrsnica
into	unutar
introduce	predstaviti
invasion	napad, upad
invitation	poziv
invite	pozvati
iron, as in metal	željezo
iron, as in for clothes	pegla
iron (v.)	peglati
is	je
island	otok

isolated	izolovan
it	to, ono
itch	svrab
its	njegov, svoj
itself	sebi, se

J

jack, for car	dizalica
jacket	jakna
jam	džem
- traffic jam	saobraćajna gužva
jealous	ljubomoran
jeans	farmerke, teksas, pamućna tkanina
jewelry	nakit
Jewish	židov, jevrej
jog, go jogging	trčanje
joke	šala
journalist	novinar
judge	sudija
journey	putovanje
jump	skok, skočati
jumpstart (dead battery)	
- can you give me a jump?	možete li prespojiti akumulator?
junk	smeće
just	
- just one	samo jedan
- just right	upravo tako
justice	pravda

K

keep	zadržati
kettle	lonac
key	ključ
kidding	šaliti

kidnap	kidnapovati
kidney	bubreg
kids	klinci
kill	ubiti
killer	ubica
kind, sort	vrsta, sorta
- which kind?	koja vrsta?
kind, nice	ljubazno
kiss	poljubac
kitchen	kuhinja
knee	koljeno
knife	nož
knitting	pletenje
knot	čvor
know	znati
Koran	Kur'an

L

ladder	stepenice, basamaci
lake	jezero
lamb	jagnje
lamp	lampa
language	jezik, govor
laptop computer	džepni kompjuter
large	velik
last, final (last dance)	posljedjni
last, past (last year)	prošli
last, enduring	trajni
- at last!	konačno!
late	kasno, zakasnio/la
- too late	prekasno
laugh	smijati se
laundry	praonica, rublja, veša
law	zakon
- against the law	protivzakonito
lawyer	advokat

lazy	lijen
lay	leći
lead (v.)	rukovođenje
lead (n.)	olovo
leader	rukovodilac
leaf	list
leak (n.)	pukotina, rupa
leak (v.)	curiti
leap	skok
learn	učiti
least	nimalo
- at least	bar
leather	koža
leave, take off	polaziti, odlaziti
leave it here/there	ostavite ovdje/tamo
- may I leave this here?	mogu li ovo ostaviti ovdje?
left, as in direction	lijevo
left, as in leave (f., m.)	otišla, otišao
leg	noga
lemon	limun
lend	pozajmiti
- would you lend me your pen?	da li biste mi posudili svoje pero?
less	manje, manji
let, allow	dopusiti
- let me go!	pustite me
- let's go	hajdemo
- will you let me...	da li biste...
- let me try	dozvolite mi da pokušam
letter	pismo
level, gradation	nivo
level, flat	ravan
liberation	oslobođenje
library	biblioteka

lie down	leći
lie, as in tell a lie	lagati
lies	laži
life	život
lift up	podići
lift, as in ride	povesti
light, as in lamp and color	svijetlo
light, as in not heavy	lagan
light bulb	sijalica
lightning	munja
lighter	upaljač
like, as in I like...	dopada mi se, volim
- do you like...?	volite li ...?
- I would like	želim (want)
- I would like (formal, f., m.)	želila bih, želio bih
- like this	ovakav
- alike	slično
lip	usna
lipstick	karmin
listen	slušati
little	malo
live	živjeti
lively person, place	živahan, živ
liver	jetra
local	lokalni
located	postaviti
lock	katanac, brava
locked	zaključano je
lonely	usamljen
long (duration)	dugo
long distance	međugradski razgovor
long ago	davno
look, appear	izgledati
look, see	gledati, pogledati
look for	tražiti
look out!	pazite

loose	labav
lose	izgubiti
- I'm lost, (f., m.)	izgubila/izgubio sam se
lot, a lot	puno, mnogo
loud	glasan
lousy	užasno
love	voliti
- I love you	volim te
- fall in love (f., m.)	zaljubljen/a
- make love	vodimo ljubav
lovely	divan
low	nizak
lower	smanjiti
lucky	sreća
- good luck!	sretno!
- just my luck!	takve sam sreće!
- pure luck	puka sreće
luggage	prtljaga
lunch	ručak
lung	pluća
luxury	luksuz

M

machine	mašina, stroj
mad (angry)	ljut
mad (crazy)	lud
mafia	mafija
magazine	časopis, magazin
mail	pošta
mailbox	poštansko sanduče
main	glavni
majority	većina
make	praviti, izraditi, raditi
male	muški
ma'am, madam	gospođa

man	muškarac, čovjek
manager	direktor
many	mnogo, puno
- too many	previše
map	karta
marital status	bračno stanje
market	trgovina
marriage (f., m.)	udaja, ženidba
married (f., m.)	udata, oženjen
marsh	močvara
matches	šibice
matter, it doesn't matter	stvar, nije važno
- what's the matter?	u čemu je stvar?
mattress	madrac
may I?	mogu li?
maybe	možda
me	
- with me	sa mnom
- for me	za mene
- it's me	to sam ja
- me, too	i ja
meal/s	objed, obroci
mean - what does it mean?	šta to znaći?
- what does this word mean?	šta znači ova riječ?
- he's mean and nasty	On je podao i grozan
meat	meso
medication	lijek
medium - sized	srednje - veličine
meet	sresti
- nice to meet you	drago mi je
- let's meet again	nađimo se ponovo
meeting	sastanak
mend	popraviti
mention - don't mention it	nema na čemu
menu	jelovnik
mess	zbrka, nered

message	poruka
- to leave a message	ostaviti poruku
midday	podne
middle	u sredini
midnight	ponoć
milk	mlijeko
mill	mlin
mind, I changed my mind (f., m.)	predomisli-la/o sam se
- would you mind if I...	imate li nešto protiv ako ja...
- I don't mind	svejedno mi je
mine, it's mine	moje, to je moje
mine, coal	rudnik
mine (explosive)	mina
miner	rudar
minority	manjina
mirror	ogledalo
miss (young woman)	gospođica
miss, I miss you	nedostajete mi
- I missed the bus	propusti-la/o sam autobus
- something's missing	nešto nedostaje
mistake	greška
misunderstanding	nesporazum
mixture	mješavina
modern	moderan
moment	trenutak
money	para, novac
month	mjesec
moon	mjesec
- full moon	pun mjesec
more	više
morning	jutro
- in the morning	ujutro
mosquito	komarac

most, majority	većina
- I like this one most	ovaj mi se sviđa najviše
- most of the time	najveći dio vremena
mother	majka
motorbike, moped	motocikl, moped
mountain	planina
mountain pass	klanac
mouse	miš
moustache	brkovi
mouth	usta
move, change homes	seliti, preseliti
move, change place	pomaknuti
movie	film
- cinema, movies	kino
much (how much, a lot)	pošto, puno
mud	blato
mule	mazga
murder	ubiti
murdered (m., f., pl.)	ubijen/a /-ni
muscle	mišić
museum	muzej
mushroom	gljiva
music	muzika
Muslim	Musliman
must	morati
mustard	senf
my	moja
myself	sebi, sebe

N

nail, finger	nokat
nail, as in hammer	ekser
naked	go
name	ime
- last name	prezime

- what's your name?	kako se zovete?
- my name is	zovem se
napkin	salveta
narrow	uzak
nasty	gadan
nation	nacija, narod
national	narodni
nationality	narodnost,
	nacionalnost
natural	prirodan
nausea	mučnina
near	blizu
nearly	gotovo
neat	uredan
necessary	potreban
neck, under your head	vrat
need (v.)	trebati
need (n.)	potreba
needle	igla
negotiator	pregovarač
neighbor	susjed, komšija
neighborhood	susjedstvo, komšiluk
neither	nijedan
nephew	nećak
nervous	nervozan
net	mreža
never	nikad
new	nov
news	vijest
newspapers	novine
New Year	Nova godina
- happy new year!	sretna nova godina
next	sljedeći
next to	pored
nice	prijatan, ljubazan
nickname	nadimak

niece	nećakinja
night	noć
nightclub	noćni-klub, disko
nightmare	noćna-mora
no	ne
- oh no!	nije valjda
nobody	niko
noise	buka
noisy	bučan
none	nijedan
nonsense	besmislica
nonsmoking	za nepušače
nor do I, nor does she	ni ja, ni ona
normal	normalan
north	sjever
nose	nos
not	ne
- not enough	nije dovoljno/dosta
nothing	ništa
now	sada
nowhere	nigdje
nuisance	gnjavaža, smetnja, muka
numb	utrnuo
number	broj
nurse	bolničarka
nuts/seeds	sjemenice

O

obligation	obaveza
observer	promatrač
obnoxious	odvratan
obvious	očigledno
occasionally	povremeno
ocean	more

odd, strange	čudan
odd, not even	neparan
of	od
off	ugašen, ugasiti
office	kancelarija, ured
official (n.)	službenik
often	često
oil	ulje, nafta (diesel)
OK	u redu
old	star
- how old are you?	koliko godina imate?
old fashioned	staromodan
old town	stari grad
olive	maslina
on	na
once	jednom
once upon a time	jednom davno, bilo jednom
one-way street	jedno-smjerna ulica
one-way ticket	karta u jednom pravcu
only	samo
open, not closed	otvoren
open (v.)	otvoriti
opening time	radno vrijeme
operation	operacija
opportunity	prilika
opposite	suprotan
opposite, across from	prekoputa
opposition (party)	opozicija (stranka)
optimistic	optimistički
optional	opcionalan
or	ili
orange (fruit)	narandža
orange (color)	narandžast
orchard	voćnjak
order (in a restaurant)	naručiti

- out of order	u kvaru je, ne radi
- everything is in order	sve je u redosljedu
ordinary	običan
organize	organizirati
original	originalan
orphan	siroče
Orthodox	Pravoslavac
other	drugi
otherwise	inače
ouch	jao!
ought	trebati
our	naš
out	van, napolje
- get out!	izlazite!
outdoors	napolju
outside	vani
oven	pećnica, rerna
over	preko, nad
- over here, over there	ovdje, tamo
- it's over, finished	je prošao
overweight	pretežak
owe	dugovati
- how much do I owe you?	koliko vam dugujem?
own	vlastiti
- my own	moj vlasiti
- on my own	sam sam
owner	vlasnik
oyster	kamenica
oxygen	kisik

P

pack, as in suitcase	spakovati
package	paket
padlock	katanac
pain	bol
painful	bolan

paint (n.)	boja
paint (v.)	slikati
painting	slika
pair	par
pajamas	pidžama
pale	blijed
pants, trousers	pantalone
panties	gaćice
pantyhose	hulahopke, najlonke
paper	papir
- piece of paper	komad papira
- newspaper	novine
pardon me? I don't understand	molim, ne razumijem
parents	roditelji
park (n.)	park
park (v.)	parkirati
parking lot	parkiralište
part (n.)	dio
partner, sweetheart	partner
partner, business	ortak
party	zabava
party, political	stranka
pass by someone	proći
passable road	prohodan
passed out	onesvijestiti se
passenger	putnik
passport	pasoš
past, not future	prošlost
past, as in walk past	proćI
pasta	tjestenina
pastime	razonoda
path	staza
patient, as in be patient	budite strpljivi
patient, as in doctor	pacijent
pay	platiti
peace and quiet	mir i tišina

peach	breskva
peanuts	kikiriki
pear	kruška
pearl	biser
peas	grašak
peasant, peasants	(impolite term) seljak, seljaci
peculiar	čudan
pedestrian	pješak
pee	pišati
pen	pero
pen pal	prijatelj za dopisivanje
pencil	olovka
people	narod, ljudi
pepper, black	biber
pepper, vegetable	paprika
percent	procenat, postotak
perfect	savršen
perhaps	možda
period of time	period
period, monthly	menstruacija
person	osoba
personal	lični
petrol, gasoline	benzin
pharmacy	apoteka
photograph	slika, snimak (shot)
photographer	fotograf
phrase	izraz
phrase book	rječnik fraza
piano	klavir
picnic	piknik
picture	slika, crtež
pie (but it's not the same)	pita
piece	komad
pig	prase, svinja

pigeon	golub
pill	pilula
pillow	jastuk
pipe	lula
pity, it's a pity	šteta
pizza, pizzeria	pica, piceria
place (n.)	mjesto
- at my place, our place	kod mene, kod nas
- place of birth	mjesto rođenja
plain, flat land	ravan
plain, not fancy	skroman
plane	avion
plant	biljka
plant seeds	sijati sjeme
plate	tanjir
platform	peron, platforma
play, as in let's	igrati se
play, as in theater	kazališni komad, predstava
playground	igralište
pleasant	prijatan, ugodan
please, as in thank you	molim
please, as in I like it	svidjeti se
pleasure	užitak
- with pleasure	sa zadovoljstvom
plum	šljiva
plus	plus
pocket	džep
point, as in finger	pokazati
point, as in meaning	svrha
point, as in numbers (5.5)	zarez, which means comma! (5,5)
poisonous	otrovan
police	milicija, policija
polish	očistiti (v), laštilo (n)
polite	učtiv (learn - učiti)

92

politician	političar
politics	politika
polluted	zagađen
pond	jezero
pony	poni
pool (swimming)	bazen
pool (billiards)	bilijar
poor	siromašan
poor (unfortunate)	jadan
popular	popularan
pork	svinjetina
posh	otmjen
possibility	mogućnost
possible	moguće
- as soon as possible	što je brze moguće
- as much as possible	što je više moguće
post	pošta
postcard	razglednica
poster	plakat
pot	lonac
potato	krompir
pottery	grnčarija, keramika
pour	proliti
power (energy)	struja
power (might)	moć
powerful	moćan
practice	vježbati
- I need to practice	treba da vježbam
precious	dragocjen
prefer	više voljeti
preferably	radije
preference	prednost
pregnant	trudna
prepare	pripremiti
prescription	recept
present (gift)	poklon

present	sada
present (v.)	predstaviti
president	predsjednik
pretty	lijep, divan
pressure	pritisak
price	cijena
pride	ponos
printer	štampač
priority	prednost
prison	zatvor
private	privatan
prize	nagrada
probably	vjerojatno
problem	problem
- no problem	nema problema
profession	profesija
promise (v.)	obečavati
promise (n.)	obećanje
pronounce	izgovoriti
- I can't pronounce it	ne mogu izgovoriti
	(bez šljivovic)
prostitute	prostitutka, kurva
protect	štititi
protection	zaštita
protest	protestirati
proud	ponosan
prunes	suhe šljive
public	javni
public holiday	državni praznik
pull	vući
punctual	tačan
pure	čist
purple	ljubičast
purse	tašna
push	gurati
put	staviti

pyjamas	pidžama

Q

quality	kvalitet
quarter	četvrt
question	pitanje
queue	red
quick	brz
quickly	brzo
quiet	mir, tišina
quit	odustati
quite	sasvim

R

rabbit	zec
rabies	bjesnilo
race (competition)	trka
race (ethnicity)	rasa
radiator	hladnjak
railway	željeznica
rain	kiša
ram	ovan
Ramadan (Muslim holiday)	Ramazan
rape	silovanje
rare, hard to find	rijedak
rat	štakor
rather, I'd rather..	radije bih.....
raw	sirov
razor	britva, žilet
read	čitati
ready	spreman
real	stvaran, pravi
really	stvarno, zaista
reason (n.)	razlog
reasonable	prihvatljiv/a, razuman
- be reasonable!	budite razumni!

recipe	recept
recognize	prepoznati
recommend	preporučiti
record (on tape)	snimak
record (file)	dosije
red	crven
Red Cross, Crescent	Crveni Krst, Polumjesec
refrigerator	frižider
refugee	izbjeglica
refugee camp	izbjeglički kamp
regime	režim
region	regija
relative	rođak (this means cousin)
relax	opustiti
relaxing	opuštajuče/a/i
remember	zapamtiti
remote	udaljeno
rent	iznajmiti
repair	popraviti
repeat	ponoviti
- can you repeat that please?	možete li to ponoviti, molim?
replace	zamijeniti
report (n.)	izvještaj, report
report (v.)	izvjestiti, prijaviti
request (n.)	zahtjev
request (v.)	zahtijevati
require	oboveza
rescue	spasiti
reservation	rezervacija
reserved	rezervisan
rest, take it easy	odmoriti
rest, take the rest	ostatak
return	povratak

return ticket	povratna karta
reverse	nazad
revolution	revolucija
rice	riža
rich	bogat
ride (n.)	vožnja
- can you give me a ride?	možete li me povesti?
ride (v.)	voziti se
ridiculous	smiješno
rifle	puška
right, not left	desno
right, as in not wrong	u pravu, tačan
ring, on finger	prsten
ring, telephone	zvono
ripe fruit	zrelo voće
risky	rizično
river	rijeka
road	put, cesta
roadblock	barikada
rob	opljačkati
robbery	pljačka
rock	stijena
roof	krov
room	soba
rope	uže, konop, špaga
rose	ruža
rough, rough road	grub put
route	pravac, smijer
rubbish	smeće
rude	neuljudan, neprijatan
ruined	srušen
ruins	ruševine
run	trčati
run!	trk!
run out of...	nestalo
rust	hrđa

S

sad	tužan
safe	siguran
safety	sigurnost
sale, for sale	prodavati, za prodaju
salt	sol
salty	slan
same	isto
sand	pijesak
sausage	kobasica
say	reći
school	škola
science	nauka
scientist	naučnik
scissors	makaze
sea	more
search	tražiti, ispitivati
season	godišnje doba, sezona
seat	mjesto
second (ord. num.)	drugi
second	sekunda
secret	tajna
security	sigurnost
see	vidjeti
seed	sjeme, klica
seek	tražiti
seldom	rijetko
sell	prodati
send	poslati
senior citizen	penzioner
sense	smisao
sensible	razuman
sensitive	osjećajan/-na
separate	razdvojeno
serious	ozbiljan

service	služba
session	sastanak
several	nekoliko
shadow	sjena
shallow	plićak
shame, what a shame!	šteta
shameful	bezobrazan
share	dijeliti
sharp	oštar
she	ona
sheep	ovca
sheet	plahta
shine	sijati
shiny	sjajan
shell	ljuska
ship	brod
shirt	košulja
shock, surprise	šok
shock, electrical	udar
shoes	cipele
shoot	pucati
- don't shoot!	ne pucaj!
shop	trgovina
shore	obala
short	kratak
show (v.)	pokazati
show (n.)	šou
shower	tuš
shut	zatvoriti
shy	stidan
sick	bolestan
sign, stopsign	znak
sign, to write your name	potpisati se
signature	potpis
sightseeing	razgledanje
silence	tišina

silver	srebro
similar	sličan
simple, easy	lako
simple, not complicated	jednostavan
since	od
sincere	iskren
sing	pjevati
single, one	jedan
single, not married	samac
sister	sestra
sit	sjediti
situation	situacija
size	veličina
skillful	spretan
skin	koža
sky	nebo
slanted	nagnut
sleep	spavati
sleepy	pospan
slim	vitak
slope	nagib
sloppy	prljav
slow	polako
small	mali
smart	inteligentan, pametan
smell, a strange smell	čudan miris
smelly	smrdi
smile	smiješiti se
smoke from fire	dim
smoke cigarettes	pušiti
smuggler	krijumčar
snack	zalogaj
snake	zmija
snow	snijeg
so	tako
so much	vrlo mnogo

soap	sapun
socks	čarape
soft	mekan
soldier	vojnik
some	neki
somehow	nekako
someone	neko
something	nešto
son	sin
song	pjesma
soon	uskoro
sorry	žao
sort, variety, kind	vrsta
soul	duša
soup	čorba, supa
sour	kiselo
sour cream	kajmak
south	jug
speak	govoriti, tell = reći, talk = pričati
speaker	govornik
special	poseban
speed	brzina
spell (say letter by letter)	govoriti slovo po slovo
spend	potrošiti
spicy	začinjen, ljut
split	podijeliti
spoiled	pokvareno
sponge	spužva
spoon	kašika
spread	mazati
spring, season	proljeće
spring, water source	izvor
spy	špijun
stamp	marka

stand up	stajati
star	zvijezda
start	početak
starving, I'm starving	gladovati, gladujem
station	stanica
statue	statua
stay	ostati
steal	krasti
steel	čelik
stick, from tree	štap, šipka
stingy	škrt
stone	kamen
stop	stati
storm	nevrijme, oluja
stove	peć
straight	ravan
strange	čudan
stranger	stranac
stream	potok
street	ulica
strength	snaga
strike, attack	napad
strike, worker	štrajk
string	kanafa, traka
strong	snažan
struggle	boriti se, borba
stuck	zaglaviti
student	student, učenik
stupid	glup
suburb	predgrađe
successful	uspješan
suddenly	iznenada
sugar	šećer
suggest	predložiti
suggestion	prijedlog
suitcase	kofer

summer	ljeto
sun	sunce
sunglasses	sunčane naočale
sunny	sunčan
sunrise	zora
sunset	zalazak sunca
surgeon	hirurg
surgery	operacija
surprise	iznenađenje
swamp	močvara
swear	kleti se
sweep	pomesti
sweet	slatka
sweetness	slatkoća
swim	plivati
swimming pool	bazen
switch off	izključiti
switch on	uključiti
swollen	otekao
sympathy	suosjećajnost
system	sistem

T

table	sto
tablet	tableta
take	uzeti
take care!	čuvati se
talk	govoriti, pričati
tall	visok
tampons	tampon, uložci
tank, reservoir	cisterna
tape	traka, kaseta
taste (n.)	okus, ukus
taste (v.)	probati, kušati
tasteless	bezukusan
tasty	ukusan

tax	porez, taksa
taxi	taksi
tea	čaj
teach	učiti, podučavati
teacher	učitelj
team	tim
tear, rip	poderati
tears, crying	suze
teaspoon	mala kašika
teeth	zubi
telephone	telefon
television	televizija
tell	reći
temperature	temperatura
tent	šator
terrible	strašan, grozan
thank (v.)	zahvaliti
thank you	hvala
that	onaj, ono, ona
thaw	topljenje
theater	kazalište, pozorište
theft	krađa
there	tamo, ondje
these	ovi, ove, ova
they	oni, one, ona
thick	debeo
thief	lopov
thin	tanak
thing	stvar, predmet (subject)
think	misliti
thirsty	žedan
this	ovaj, ova, ono
those	oni, one, ona
throw, throw away	baciti
throw up	povraćati

thumb	palac
thunder	grom
ticket	karta
ticket office	blagajna
tie	kravata
tie up	svezati
tight	tijesan
time	vrijeme
tip, restaurant	napojnica
tire (n.)	gume na točkovima
tired	umoran
tissue	maramica
tobacco	duhan
today	danas
toe	nožni prst
together	zajedno
toilet	WC (vey-tsey)
tomato	paradajz
tomb	grob
tomorrow	sutra
tonight	večeras
too	suviše, previše
tooth	zub
toothache	zubobolja
toothbrush	četkica za zube
toothpaste	pasta za zube
top	vrh
torture	mučenje, tortura
total	ukupno
touch	dodir
tough	žilav
tourist	turista
towards	prema
towel	peškir, ručnik
tower	kula, toranj
town	grad

traffic	saobračaj
traffic jam	zastoj saobraćaja
traffic light	semafor
train	voz, vlak
train station	željeznička stanica
translate	prevesti
translator	prevodilac
trauma	šok, trauma
travel	putovati
traveller	putnik
treacherous	izdajnički
tree	stablo
trouble	nezgoda
trousers	pantalone
truce	primirje
truck	kamion
true	istinit
truth	istina
try	probati
turkey	puran, ćuran
turn, it's my turn	red
turn around	okrenuti
turn left/right	skreni lijevo/desno
twice	dva put
twins	blizanci
typical	tipičan

U

ugly	ružan
ulcer	čir
umbrella	kišobran
uncomfortable	neudoban
under	dolje, ispod
understand	razumjeti
unemployed	nezaposlen
unfair	nepravedno

106

unfortunately	na žalost
unfriendly	neprijazan
unhappy	nesretan, jadan
unhealthy	nezdrav
union, trade union	ujedinjenje
United Nations	Ujedinjene Nacije
university	univerzitet
until	do, dok
unusual	neobičan
up	gore, naviše
urgent	hitan
us	nas
use	upotrijebiti
useful	koristan
usual	običan
usually	obično
U-turn	promjena pravca

V

vacancies at a hotel	slobodnih soba
vacation	raspust
vaccinate	vakcinacija
- I have been vaccinated	ja sam vakcinisan
valley	dolina
valuable	dragocjen
valuables	dragocjenosti
value (n.)	vrijednost
vase	vazna
veal	teletina
vegetables	povrće
vegetarian	vegetarijanka
venereal disease	spolna bolest
very	veoma, vrlo
via	preko
view	vidik, pogled
village	selo

vine	loza
vinegar	sirće
violence	nasilje
visa	viza, dozvola
visability	vidljivost
visit	posjetiti
visitor	posjetilac
vital	bitno je da
voice	glas
vomit	povračati
vote	glas

W

wage, salary	nadnica
wage, war	voditi rat
wait	čekati
wake up	probuditi se
walk	hodati, šetati
wallet	novčanik
walnut	orah
wander	lutati
want	željeti
war	rat
war crimes	ratni zločini
warm	toplo
warn	upozoriti
wash	prati (se)
waste	neupotrebljiv
wasteful	rasipno
watch, look	oprezati, gledati
water	voda
waterfall	vodopad
watermelon	lubenica
way	put, cesta
- this way	ovaj put
we	mi

weak	slab
wear	nositi
weather	vrijeme
wedding	vjenčanje
week	sedmica
weekend	vikend
weight	težina
welcome	dobrodošao
well, good	dobro
well (n.)	zdenac
west	zapad
wet	mokar, vlažan
what	što, šta
wheat	pšenica
wheel	točak
when	kada
where	gdje
which	koji
white	bijelo
who	ko
whole	cijeli, potpun
why	zašto
wide	širok
widow	udovica
wife	žena, supruga
wild, not tamed	divlji
win	pobijediti
- who won?	ko je pobijedio?
wind, as in blows	vjetar, dah
window	prozor
windy	vjetrovit
wine	vino
winter	zima
wisdom	mudrost
wish	željeti
with	sa

without	bez
wolf	vuk
womb	maternica
women	žena
wonderful	divan
wood and woods	šuma
wool	vuna
work	posao, rad
world	svijet
worried	zabrinut
worse	lošiji
wristwatch	straža
write	pisati
wrong	neprav

X

x ray	x zraci
xylophone	ksilofon

Y

yard	dvoršte
year	godina
yellow	žuto
yes	da
yesterday	juče
yet	stiglo
- not yet	još nije
yogurt	jogurt
you	ti(fam), tebe(obj), vi(pl), vas (obj)
young	mlad
younger person who must respect older ones	balavica
youth hostel	omladinski hotel
your, yours	tvoj (fam), vaš (pl)

Z

zero	nula
zoo	zoološki vrt

Arrival, Meeting and Greeting
Dođi, upoznaj i razgovaraj

Good morning!	Dobro jutro!
Good afternoon!	Dobar dan!
Good evening!	Dobro veče!
Good night!	Laku noć!
Sleep well!	Dobro spavajte!
Hi!	Zdravo!
What's up?	Šta ima?
(familiar greeting)	Gdje si?
(answer to above)	Evo me! or Tu sam!
	or Ovdje!
How are you?	Kako si? Kako ste?
I'm fine, and you?	Dobro, a vi?
Not bad	Nije loše
What is your name?	Kako se zovete?
My name is	Moje ime je/ja se
	zovem
Where are you from?	Odakle ste
I'm from...	Ja sam iz
☐ America	Amerike
☐ England	Engleske
☐ Germany	Njemačke
☐ France	Francuske
☐ Canada	Kanade
Do you speak English?	Govorite li Engleski?
☐ German?	Njemacki?
☐ French?	Francuski?
I don't speak Bosnian	Ja ne govorim
	Bosanski
I only speak a little Bosnian.	Ja govorim malo
	Bosanski
Just a minute	Čekaj! or Sačekaj!
I'd like you to meet my...	Želim vas upoznati sa
	mojim/mojom. . .

113

('m' at the end denotes possession)

☐ husband	mužem
☐ wife	ženom
☐ boyfriend	dečkom, momkom
☐ girlfriend	djevojkom, curom
☐ friend	prijatéljem (m), prijateljicom (f)
☐ colleague	kolegom, drugom, saradnikom
What do you do? je	Šta radite? Koje vam zanimanje?
I'm a ...	Ja sam...
☐ teacher	učitelj
☐ doctor	doktor, liječnik
☐ nurse	bolničarka, medicinska sestra
☐ therapist	terapeut
☐ economist	ekonomista
☐ architect	arhitekta
☐ lawyer	advokat, pravnik
☐ student	učenik (in school)
student (in	university)
☐ journalist	novinar
I'm with... (OSCE, IFOR, etc)	Ja sam sa (OSCE, IFOR, etc)-om
Pleased to meet you!	Drago mi je da vas upoznajem!
Good-bye!	Doviđenja!
See you tomorrow!	Vidimo se sutra!
It was nice meeting you!	Bilo mi je drago!
Thank you	Hvala
Please	Molim vas
You're welcome	Nema na čemu, molim
Welcome!	Dobro došli!
Bon voyage!	Sretan put

114

Come again!	Dođite opet!
Good luck!	Sretno
May I?	Mogu li?
Yes	Da
No	Ne
Excuse me	Izvinite
Sorry!	Oprosti, žao mi je
How old are you?	Koliko godine imate?
I am...years old	Ja imam ____ godina
Here you are	Izvolite
Where do you live?	Gdje živite?
My goodness/I swear!	Bogami! Kunem se!
I'm just kidding!	Ja se samo šalim!
	Šalim se
Its finished	Gotovo je
so...	dakle...
also...	takođe
Where are you going?	Kuda idete? or Gjde ideš?
Lets go!	Hajdemo!
Go away!	Gubi se!
you should...	Treba li...
How do you say this?	Kako kažeš?
how many	koliko
(slang for) how much money	pošto
what kind?	kakva vrsta?
at what time?	u koliko sati?
when	kada
which one	koji
why	zašto
because	zato što
excuse me	izvinite
I'm sorry	Žao mi je, oprostite

it's too bad	šteta
never mind	ništa zato, nema veze, nije važno
bless you (post-sneeze)	nazdravlje!
I don't believe you	Ne vjerujem
I don't know (anything)	Ne znam (ništa)
I don't know what to do	Ne znam šta da radim
That's interesting	To je zanimljivo, interesantno
I (don't) understand	(ne) razumjem
I forgot	zaboravi-la/-o sam
I remember	pamtim
of course	naravno
that's---	to je ---
It's true	Istina-je
Just my luck!	Takve sam sreće!
At last!	Konačno!
It won't work, It's not right	Ne valja!
Are you comfortable?	Jeli ti ugodno?
Come stay with us!	Dođi kod nas u goste!
like that	tako
over there	tamo
here	to, ovdje
Did you make that?	Da li si ti ovo napravi-o/la?
for sure	sigurno
I agree	Slažem se
I'll show you	Ja ću ti pokazati
show me	pokaži mi
You're right!	U pravu si
You're wrong!	Nisi u pravu
I'm ready.	Ja sam spreman/na
Come in!	Uđi!

That's all!	To je sve!
look out!	pazite!
look!	pogledaj!
you are lying!	lažeš!
shut up!	zaveži!
be quiet!	smiri se!
explicative	stranje! jebiga!
a lot	puno, mnogo
several	nekoliko
a little	malo
someone	neko
everyone	svako
no one	niko
sometimes	ponekad
always	uvijek
never	nikad
somewhere	negdje
everywhere	svuda
nowhere	nigdje
everything	sve
something	nešto
nothing	ništa
every	svaki
come here	dođi ovamo
come back!	vrati se!
come with me	podji sa mnom
Please correct me if I make a mistake.	Ispravi me ako griješim.
Can you explain that to me?	Možete li mi to objasniti?

Let's go somewhere else.	Hajdemo na neko
drugo mjesto.	
This has been an	
unforgetable experience!	Ovo je bilo
nezaboravno iskustvo!	
I've had a wonderful time!	Bila mi je lijepo!

Accommodation

I am looking for a hotel.	Ja tražim hotel
Is there anywhere I/we	Ima li negdje za mene/nas
can stay for the night?	prenoćište?
Where is a... hotel?	Gdje .... hotel?
- cheap	- jeftin
- good	- dobar
- nearby	- blizu
- clean	- čist
What is the address?	Koja je adresa?
Could you write it down please? napisati	Možete li molim vas adresu?

At the hotel

Do you have any rooms tonight?	Imate li neku for slobodnu sobu?
I would like a ...	Ja bih želio (or - želila)....
single room	- jedno-krevetnu sobu
- double room	- dvo-krevetnu sobu
We'd like a room.	Mi želimo sobu.
I want a room with a ...	Želim sobu sa...
- bathroom	- WC (vey-tsay)
- shower	- tušom
- balcony	- balkonom
I want a quiet room.	Želim mirnu sobu.
How much is it per night/ per person?	Koliko košta noć/za jedno?
How much is it per week?	Koliko košta sedmično?
How long will you be staying?	Koliko dugo ćete ostati?

119

How many nights?	Koliko noći?
It's ... per day / per person	To je.... po danu / po osobi.
I'm staying for..	Ja ću ostati...
- one day	- jedan dan
- two days	- dva dana
- one week	- jednu sedmicu
Can I see the room?	Mogu li vidjeti sobu?
Are there any others?	Imate li još neke sobe?
Is there ...?	Ima li tamo...?
- air conditioning	- klima uredaj
- laundry service	- vešeraj
- room service	- sobna usluga
- a telephone	- telefon
- hot water	- topla voda
No, I don't like it.	Ne, ne sviđa mi se.
It's too...	Previše je....
- cold	- hladno
- hot	- toplo
- big	- veliko
- small	- malo
- dark	- tamno
- dirty	- prljavo
- noisy	- bučno
It's fine, I'll take it.	Dobro je, uzet ću je.
Where's the bathroom?	Gdje je WC?
Is there hot water all day?	Ima li tople vode cijeli dan?
Is there anyplace to wash clothes?	Ima li se negdje oprati odjeća?
Can I use the telephone?	Mogu li koristiti telefon?

Do you have any ID?	Imate li neki dokument?
Sorry, we're full.	Žalim, mi smo puni.
I have a reservation.	Ja imam rezervaciju.
My name is...	Moje ime je....
	-Zovem se ....
May I speak to the manager please?	Molim vas mogu li govoriti sa šefom?
I'm meeting someone here.	Ja imam susret snekim ovdje.

I need...
- candles
- toilet paper
- soap
- clean sheets/towels
- another blanket
- drinking water
- a light bulb

Ja trebam...
- svijeće
- toalet papir
- sapun
- čiste plahte/peškire
- posebnu deku
- pitku vodu
- sijalicu

Please wake me up at..	Molim probudite me u...
I want a wake up call.	Želim buđenje.
Please change the sheets.	Molim promjenite posteljinu.
I can't open/close the window.	Ni mogu otvoriti/zatvoriti prozor.
I've lost my key	Ja sam izgubio ključ.
Can I have the key to my room?	Mogu li dobiti ključ od moje sobe?
The toilet won't flush.	Vodokotlić ne radi.
There is no water.	Nema vode.
There is no electricity.	Nema struje.
The heater doesn't work.	Grijanje ne radi

What is your room number?	Koji je broj tvoje sobe?

I'm leaving now	Odlazim sada.
We are leaving now	odlazimo sada.
I would like to pay the bill.	Ja želim platiti račun.
Is it included?	Je li to uključeno?

Restaurants and Food

Ways to order -

Do you like...?	Volite li...?
I like	Volim / dopada mi se
I don't like	Ja ne volim / ne dopada mi se
I prefer	Više volim
I don't eat	Ja ne jedem
May I have	Mogu li imati
Can you	Možete li
I can/I can't	Mogu / ne mogu
Could I have	Mogu li dobiti
I'd like	Želio bih (m) - željela bih (f)
Do you have	Imate li
What is this?	Što je ovo?
Is it spicy?	To je ljuto/začinjeno?
What is it made of?	Sa čim je pravljeno?
Does it have meat in it?	Ima li mesa? - or - Je li sa mesom?
I am a vegetarian.	Ja sam vegetarijanka
I would like something without meat.	Ja želim neko jelo bez mesa.
What do you have?	Šta imate?
I have diabetes.	Ja imam šečernu bolest.
Which items on this menu are available today?	Što imate danas na jelovniku?
What do you recommend?	Šta preporucujete?
Okay	U redu
That's enough, thanks	Dosta je, hvala
A little more, please	Još malo, molim
Just a little, please	Samo malo, molim

some	neki
a lot	puno, mnogo
too much	previše
no more	nema više
I'm hungry	Gladan sam - gladna sam
I'm thirsty	Žedan sam - žedna sam
Bon apetite!	Prijatno!
I'm full	Sit/a sam
Check please!	Račun, molim
It was delicious, thank you	Bilo je veoma ukusno, hvala

Questions or answers you might get from the wait-staff

We don't have that item today.	Nemamo to na jelovniku danas
What would you like to eat/drink?	Šta želite jesti/piti?
We recommend ...	Preporučujemo...
We have...	Imamo....
This has meat in it.	Ima mesa unutra.
Would you like anything else?	Da li želite jos nesto?
Would you care for dessert?	Što želite slatko?

Words pertaining to food

Nouns

bowl	glava
breakfast	doručak
cafe - bar	kafić - kafana
cup	šoljica
fork	viljuška
glass of water	čaša vode
knife	nož
lunch	ručak

124

menu	jelovnik
napkin	zdjela
nonalcoholic restaurant	aščinica
pizzeria	picerija
plate	tanjir
restaurant	restoran
snack	užina
spoon	kašika
supper	večera
table for two/four	sto za dvoje/četvero
waiter/waitress	konobar/ica
wine list	vinska karta

Meat	**Meso**
beef	govedina
chicken	piletina
fish	riba
pork	svinjetina
rabbit	zec
veal	teletina
other kinds of meat	ćevapčići, puran, ćurka, šunka

Vegetables	**Povrće**
bean	grah
cabbage	kupus
carrot	mrkva
cauliflower	karfiol
corn	kukuruz
cucumber	krastavac
eggplant	patlidžan
garlic	bijeli-luk
lettuce	salata
mushroom	gljiva, pečurka
onion	luk
parsley	peršun

peas	grašak
peppers	paprika
potato	krompir
pumpkin	tikva
red onion	crni-luk
spinach	špinat
tomatoes	paradajz

Fruit	Voče
apples	jabuka
apricot	kajsija
bananas	banana
blackberry	kupina
blueberry	borovnica
cherries	trešnja
fig	smokva
grapes	grožđe
orange	naranđa
peaches	breskva
pears	kruška
plums	šljiva
quince	dunja
raisins	suho grožđe
raspberry	malina
sour cherry	višnja
strawberry	jagoda

Other foods or food terms	
bread	hljeb
butter	maslac
cheese	sir
eggs	jaje
flour	brašno
honey	med
jam	džem, pekmez

lard	maslo
milk	mlijeko
mustard	senf
pepper	papar or biber
pickled	kisela
rice	riža
salt	so or sol
sour cream	kajmak
sugar	šećer
yogurt	jogurt (not a fruited
dessert but a	sour drink or
condiment)	

Drinks	**Piti**
beer	pivo
coffee	kafa, kahva
juice	sok gusti
slivovitz	šljivovica
soft drinks	sok
tea	čaj
water	voda, kisela voda
wine	vino

Soups	**Čorba**
fish	riblja
meat	begova
mushroom	od gljiva

Main courses

Pita - this is like a cinnamon roll but not sweet. It is made with a variety of fillings such as...
sa krompirom, sirom, etc (with potatoes, cheese, etc)

pita with spinach	zeljanica
pita with meat	burek
omelette	omlet
macaroni with cheese	makaroni sa sirom

Side dishes
french fries	pomfrit
salad	salat
- green	zelena
- mixed	miješana

Also check the list of vegetables...

Desserts — **Slatko**
apple pie (also check list of fruit)	pita od jabuka
baklava	baklava
cake	torta, kolač
crepes	palačinka
ice cream	sladoled

To eat - jesti
jedem, jedeš, jede, jedemo, jedete, jedu

To drink - Piti
pijem, piješ, pije, pijemo, pijete, piju

To pay - platiti
platim, platiš, plati, platimo, platite, plate

With......
jam - sa džemom
cheese - sa sirom
chocolate - sa čokoladom
meat - sa mesom
potatoes - sa krumpirom
walnuts - sa orasima

Without....
meat - bez mesa
sugar - bez šećera

Tipping customs - no set amount, but for good service, some small token should be given. It is a wise habit to double check the bill for accuracy.

Most restaurants take either Dinar and DM. In Republika Srpska, use their currency, and in some parts of the federation with a major Croatian influence, use kuna or DM.

There is no such thing as a nonsmoking section.

Traveling Around...

Bosnia is a very beautiful country, with a large portion comprised of hills, farmland, fields, and forests. There are flat parts, too, such as the area along the Sava River around Orašje and Brčko. Best of all are the old parts of towns, nestled in the center surrounded by buildings of, say, a more utilitarian sort of architecture. There are a few castles and forts, but the mosques and churches are perhaps the most beautiful buildings. Don't let the destruction get you down. And beware of hiking far off the beaten path, those 6 to 8 million landmines haven't all been found yet. But the people are very friendly and willing to show you the local places of interest...

Directions

I'm lost!	Izgubio sam se!
Where is....	Gdje je...?
a bank	banka
the church	crkva
the Ministry of ..	ministarstvo...
the mosque	džamija
the city center	centar grada
the _____ embassy	... ambasada
my hotel	moj hotel
the market	trgovina, dučan
the museum	muzej
the police station	policija
the post office	pošta
a toilet	wc(vay-tsay), zahod
the university	univerzitet
the airport	aerodrom
the train station	željeznička stanica
the bus stop	autobuska stanica
What_____ is this?	Koji_____ je ovo?
bridge	most

building	zgrada
district	dio grada, kvart
river	rijeka
road/street	put/ulica
town	grad
village	selo
Can you show me	Možete li me pokazati
neke some places of interest?	znamenitosti?
What is that/this...	Koja je ono/ovo...?
Can I park here?	Mogu li parkirati ovdje?
Are we on the right road for...? putu za...?	Jesmo li na pravom
How many km is it to...?	Koliko kilometara ima do...?
It is _____ km.	Ima ___ kilometara.
How far is the next village?	Koliko ima do slijedečeg sela?
I'm looking for this address.	Tražim ovu adresu.
How much farther is it?	Kado ćemo tamo stiće/doći
Can you show me on the map?	Možete li mi pokazati na karti?
How do I get to...?	Kako ću doči do....
I want to go to...	Ja želim ići do...
I just want to explore.	Ja samo želim razgledati.
Can I walk there?	Mogu li tamo pješke?
Is it near/far?	Je li blizu/daleko?
It's not far.	Nije daleko
Go straight ahead	Idite samo ravno
We're almost there!	Skorosmo stigli/došli!
It's _____blocks down	To je ___ bloka/ulice dalje.
Turn left/right	Skreni lijevo/desno

at the next corner.	na slijedećem uglu/čošku
at the traffic lights.	na semaforu
A little further..	malo dalje
Up/down the hill.	uzbrdo - nizbrdo
opposite (on the other side)	prekoputa
next to	pored
crossroads	raskrsnica
one-way street	jedno-smjerna ulica
north	sjever
south	jug
east	istok
west	zapad

More Prepositions - keep in mind that using these will change the endings of words associated with them! There are so many exceptions and other grammatical rules that it becomes too complicated to explain it all here. My Bosnian friends assured me that using an incorrect ending would not hamper the message getting through...

about	oko, skoro (most objects will end in -ske)
above	iznad
after	poslije
among	između, među
at someone's place	kod
before	prije
behind	iza
between	između
beyond	preko
except	sem, izuzeti
for	za
from	od

in front of	ispred
on	na
our place	kod nas
since	od
through	kroz
to/at/into	u (most objects will end with -u)
towards	ka, prema
under	ispod
until	do, dok
until when?	dokle?
with	sa, s (most objects will end in -om)
without	bez

On the road...

hitchhiking	putovati autostopom (autostop)
Where are you going?	Gdje idete?
I'm going to...	Ja idem u...
Can you give me a lift to town?	Možete li me povesti u gradu?
Thanks for the ride!	Hvala na vožnji!
What is the name of this town?	Kako se zove ovaj grad?
How many people live there?	Koliko ljudi živi ondje?
What is the name of that river?	kako se zove ta rijeka?
- lake?	jezero
- mountain?	planina
How deep is it?	koliko je duboka?
How high is it?	koliko je visoka?
Where is the border?	Gdje je granica?
checkpoint	kontrolni punkt
roadblock	barikada

No Entry	Zabraljen ulaz
No admission	Zabraljen pristup
Emergency exit	izlaz za nuždu
Is the road passable?	Je li put prohodan?
We are repairing the ...	Mi popravljamo ...
bridge, road, house	most, put, kuća
We need gasoline.	Mi trebamo benzina.
Are there any mines nearby?	Ima li mina u blizini?
minefield	minsko polje
refugee camp	izbjeglićki kamp
relief aid	humanitarna pomoć
danger	opasnost
Be careful!	Paziti! Budite
oprezni! Budite	pažljivi
dangerous	opasan

Public Transportation

Bosnia, like all of Yugoslavia, Eastern Europe, Western Europe, Asia... well, okay, the whole world outside of North America, has a wonderfully well thought-out public transportation system. Unfortunately, it, like everything else, suffered tremendously during the war. Now there are few trains, and the buses are all pretty crowded and rundown. It was a day for celebrating when the trams in Sarajevo started running again, shrapnel marks and all. But it's cheaper than renting a car, and perhaps safer, too. Driving in Bosnia is no joke - with narrow, winding roads full of slow moving vehicles (horse carts, smelly trucks, bicycles, Fičas...). Not to mention the possibility of landmines and car-jackers. In the winter, the roads aren't well plowed or sanded. And that's just the paved roads! Most are dirt roads full of pot-holes. Which brings me back to using public transportation...

Which bus goes to...	Koji autobus ide...

135

When does the bus leave for...	Kada kreće autobus za...?
When is the next bus?	Kada je slijedeći bus?
I don't know.	Ne znam.
How long does it take to get there?	Koliko treba vremena do tamo?
What time will we arrive?	U koje vrijeme ćemo doći?
How much is the fare?	Kokliko kosta karta?
Does it go direct?	Ide li directno?
Will I need to change buses/trains?	Moram li presjedati autobus/voz?
Where will I need to change?	Gdje ću presjedati?
bus stop	autobuski stop
bus station	autobuski stanica
train	voz
train station	željeznička stanica
ticket	karta
conductor	kondukter
driver	vozač
schedule	vozni red
arrival	dolazak
departure	polazak
Sort of a mini-bus thing	kombi
taxi	taksi
entrance	uzlaz
exit	izlaz
Could you tell me when to get off?	Možete li reći kada da izađem?
I want to go to...	Želim ići u ...
Do you go to...?	Idete li u...?
Can you pick me up?	Hoćete li doći po mene?
Ticket please!	Kartu, molim!
Where can I put my bag?	Gdje mogu staviti moju torbu?

136

TRAVELING AROUND

Next stop:...	Slijedeča stanica:...
Last stop!	posljednja stanica!
All aboard!	Polazak!
The bus/train is leaving!	Bus/voz polazi!!
rest stop	pauza
How long is the rest stop?	Koliko traje pauza?
Bon voyage!	Sretan put!

Communications

Using the Phone

Where is a telephone?	Gdje je telefon?
May I use the phone?	Mogu li se poslužiti telefonom?
Can you help me with this call?	Trebam vašu pomoć da nazovem.
I'd like to make a phone call.	Želim napraviti telefonski posiv
I'd like to send a fax.	Želim poslati faks
I want to call.....	Ja želim zvati....
What is the code for....	Koji je pozivni broj za......
The number is....	Broj je....
Extension	Lokal
It's busy	zauzeto
I've been cut off	Ja imam prekid
The lines are down	Linije su prekinute
Hello! (when answering phone)	Molim! Halo!
I'd like to speak to.....	Voljela/volio bih govoriti sa....
Is _____ there?	Možete li mi dati...?
This is _____	Ovdje je_____
S/he's not here.	On/a nije tu.
Can I leave a message?	Mogu li ostaviti poruku?
When will s/he be back?	Kada će on/a doći?

In the Post Office

Where is the post office?	Gdje je pošta?
What time does the post office open?	U koliko sati se pošta otvara?
What time does it close?	U koliko sati se zatvara?

139

Where is a mail box?	Gdje je poštansko sanduče?
Is there any mail for me?	Ima li pošte za mene?
How long will it take to get there?	Koliko dugo ce putovati pošiljka?
How much does it cost?	Koliko košta pošiljka?
I would like to send...	Ja želim poslati
Air mail	Avionska pošiljka
letter - parcel/package	pismo - paket
I would like some stamps	Ja želim kupiti marku

Advanced Conversation...
What do you say after "Hello"?
(Note: written in the formal/plural form)

Family

Are you married?	Jeste li udati?
	(to a woman)
	Jeste li oženjeni?
	(to a man)
I am single.	Ja sam neudata
	(a woman says)
	Ja sam neoženjen
	(a man says)
I am married.	Ja sam udata (you can guess the rest...)
	Ja sam oženjen
I am divorced.	Ja sam razvedena
	Ja sam razveden
I am widowed.	Ja sam udovica
	Ja sam udovac
Do you have a boyfriend?	Imate li momka/dečka?
Do you have a girlfriend?	Imate li djevojku/curu?
What is his/her name?	Kako je jegovo/njeno ime?
Do you have children?	Imate li djece?
How many children do you have?	Koliko djece imate?
I don't have any children.	Ja nemam djece.
I have a daughter.	Ja imam kčerku
I have a son.	Ja imam sina
How many sisters do you have?	Koliko sestara imate?
How many brothers do you have?	Koliko braće imate?
aunt	tetka
boy	momak
brother	brat

141

children	dijete
cousin	rođak, rodica
daughter	kčerka
family	familija, porodica
father	otac
grandfather	djed
grandmother	baka
girl	djevojka
husband	muž, suprug
man	čovjek, muškarac
mother	mati, majka
parents	roditelji
people	narod, ljudi (caution: crazy=lud, angry= ljut)
person	osoba
sister	sestra
son	sin
twins	blizanci
uncle	ujak, stric (sounds like streets)
wife	žena, supruga
woman	žena

Pastimes	**Razonoda**
What do you do in your free time?	Šta radite u slobodno vrijeme?
I like to ... / Do you like to...?	Ja volim... / Volite li ...?
- bike	voziti bicikl
- dance	plesati
- drive	voziti
- fish	ribolov
- go boating	ići brodom - čamcem
- go out with my friends	ići sa prijateljima
- go shopping	ići u kupovinu

142

- go to bars	ići u bar
- go to concerts	ići na koncerte
- hike	pješačiti
- play basketball	igrati košarku
- play cards	igrati karte
- play chess	igrati šah
- play handball	igrati rukomet
- play pool	igrati bilijar
- play soccer	igrati nogomet
- play sports	igrati sport
- play volleyball	igrati odbojku
- sing	pjevati
- skate	klizati
- ski	skijati
- sleep (ho-hum)	spavati
- swim	plivati
- travel	putovati
- visit my family	posjetiti moju porodicu
- watch TV (heaven forbid)	gledati TV
- work in the garden	raditi u vrtu/bašti

On some evenings a common pastime is for all the young people to do the (environmentally sound) equivalent of dragging main--walking up and down some given road in town. They see their friends, see who their friends are with, meet new people in town, etc. This is called korziranje. The verb: Korzirati, the street: Korzo

What kind of ..... do you like?	Koju vrstu ... vi volite?
- animals	životinja
- books	knjiga
- cars	kola, auto
- clothes	odječe
- food	hrane

143

- ice cream	sladoleda
- movies	filmova
- music	muzike
- sports	sporta

What/who is your favorite...?	Šta/ko je vaš najdraži...?
- kind of food	vrsta hrane
- movie star	glumac
- place to go	mjesto za ići
- restaurant	restoran
- singer	pjevać
- song	pjesma
I like ...	Ja volim...
I don't like...	Ja ne volim...
Have you ever been to....?	Da li ste ikada bili u...?
Have you ever seen...?	Da li ste ikada vidjeli...?
Have you ever heard...?	Da li ste ikada slušali...?
Have you ever tried .....?	Da li ste ikada probali...?

Any good traveler will always bring a good book, a deck of cards, and an assortment of photos to share...

Would you like	Želite li vidjeti neke
to see some photos?	fotografije/slike?
This is my...	Ovo je moja...
- dog / cat	- pas, mačka
- car	- auto
- family	- familja, porodica
- favorite place	- najdraže mjesto
- friend	- prijatelj, prijateljica
- home	- kuća

144

- home town	- rodni grad
Do you have any photos?	Imate li vi sliku?
That's nice!	To je lijepo!
That's beautiful!	To je divno!
That's interesting!	To je interasantno
What's/who's that?	Što / ko je to?
Where did you take this photo?	Gdje si slikao ove slike?
When did you take this photo?	Kada si slikao ove slike?
I really like them!	Stvarno mi se sviđaju!
Thank you for showing me!	Hvala što ste mi pokazali.

Weather — **Vrijeme**

It's hot today.	Danas je vruće
cold	zima, hladno
nice	lijepo
sunny	sunčano
cloudy	oblačno
icy	klizavo
It's raining!	Kiša pada
It's snowing!	Snijeg pada
What's the temperature?	Kolika je temperatura?

Feelings and adjectives

I am...	Ja sam...
Are you...?	Da li si ti....?
	Da li ste vi....?
I feel...	Ja osjećam...
How do you feel?	Kako se osječate?
afraid	uplašen/uplašena
angry	ljut/ljuta
annoyed	ljutit/ljutita
ashamed	postiđen/postiđena

145

betrayed	izdajnik
bored	dosadan/dosadna
comfortable	ugodno mi je
confident	pouzdan/pouzdana
confused	smetan, zbunjen, smušen/na
disappointed	razočaran/razočarana
disgusted	gadljiv/gadljiva
excited	uzbuđen/uzbuđena
exhausted	iscrpljen/iscrpljena
frustrated	pokvaren/pokvarena
happy	sretan/sretna
homesick	čeznuti
hopeful	pun nade
hopeless	očajan/očajna
hurt	ozlijeđen/ozlijeđena
jealous	jubomoran/jubomorna
lonely	osamljen/osamljena
lousy	ušljiv/ušljiva
mystified	obmanut, zavaran/na
patriotic	rodoljub
pleased	sviđa
proud	ponosan/ponosna
sad	tužan/tužna
shocked	potrešen/potrešena
surprised	iznenađen/iznenađena
tired	umoran/umorna
uncomfortable	neugodno mi je
worried	zabrinut/zabrinuta
ambitious	ambiciozan/na
assertive	odlučan/na
capable	sposoban/na
cheerful	veseo/vesela
courteous	pristojan/na
creative	kreativan/na

creative	kreativan/na
determined	odlučan/na
easy going	relaksiran/na
enthusiastic	entuzijasta
friendly	prijateljski
	raspoložen/a
honest	iskren/a
organized	organiziran/na
patient	strpljiv/a
reliable, dependable	savjestan/na
resourceful	maštovit/a
responsible	odgovoran/na
thorough	precizan/na

determined	odlučan/na
easy going	relaksiran/na
enthusiastic	entuzijasta
friendly	prijateljski
	raspoložen/a
honest	iskren/a
organized	organiziran/na
patient	strpljiv/a
reliable, dependable	savjestan/na
resourceful	maštovit/a
responsible	odgovoran/na
thorough	precizan/na

Helpful Words

Opposites

cool - warm	hladno - toplo
forward - back	naprijed - nazad
happy - sad	radostan - tužan
healthy - sick	zdrav - bolestan
here - there	ovamo - tamo
inside - outside	unutra - napolju
left - right	lijevo - desno
little - big	mali - veliki
lucky - unlucky	srećan - nesrećan
pretty - ugly	lijep - ružan
rich - poor	bogat - siromašan
short - tall	nizak - visok
slow - fast	polako - brzo
thin - fat	mršav - debeo
up - down	gore - dole
weak - strong	slab - jak

Comparatives & Superlatives

Basic Rules of Thumb:

To make the comparative, add the suffix *-iji*;

To make the superlative, add the prefix *naj-*

Here are some examples and exceptions:

good - better - best	dobar - bolji - najbolji
bad - worse - worst	loš - lošiji - najlošiji
pretty.....	lijep - ljepši - najljepši
ugly....	ružan - ružniji - najružniji
strong...	jak - jači - najjači
small....	malo - manji - najmanji
big...	velik - veće - najveće

149

More adjectives... remember to change -an to -na if it is a female you are describing!

cheap	jeftin
clever/cunning	lukav
cold	zima, hladno
crazy	lud
cute, sweet	slatko/a
dead	mrtav
delicious	ukusan
different	različiti
difficult	teško
easy	lako
exciting	uzbudljiv
expensive	skupa
expert	struč-njak
fast	brzo
funny	šaljiv
horrible	grozan
hot	vruće
hungry	gladan
important	važan
impossible	nemoguč
lucky	sreće
married	oženjen, udati
naughty	nestašan
normal	normalan
old	stari
polite	učtiv
poor	siromašan
rich	bogat
same	isto
serious	ozbiljan
similar	sličan
single	ne-oženjen, ne-udata
sleepy	pospan

slow	polako, istpoistiha (local dialect)
strange	čudan
stupid	glup
thirsty	žedan
trickster	lopov
unfortunate	jadan
weak	slab
young	mladi

Adverbs

really	zaista, stvarno
very	vrlo, veoma

Colors

black	crna
blue	plava
brown	braon
gray	siva
green	zelena
orange	naranđasta
pink	ružičasta
purple	ljubičasta
red	crvena
white	bijela
yellow	žuta

Shopping
(the grease that keeps those wheels of captialism turning...)

Where can I buy...?	Gdje mogu kupiti...?
Where's the market?	Gdje je trgovina?
Can you help me?	Možete li mi pomoći?
I'm just looking.	Ja samo gledam.
I'd like to buy...	Ja želim kupiti...
Do you have any...?	Imate li...?
Can I look at it?	Mogu li pogledati?
this, these	ovaj, ove
that, those	onaj, tai - one
I don't like it.	Ne sviđa mi se.
I like it.	Sviđa mi se.
Do you have anything cheaper?	Imate li nešto jeftinije?
better - larger - smaller	bolji - veći - manji
Do you have anything else?	Imate li nešto drugo?
I'll take it.	To ću uzeti.
How much is it?	Koliko to košta?
Can you write down the price?	Možete li napisati cijenu?
Could you lower the price?	Možete li smanjiti cijenu?
I don't have much money.	Nemam puno para.
Thank you, good-bye!	Hvala, doviđenja
I want to return this.	Ja želim ovo vratiti.

From the shop keeper...

Can I help you?	Mogu li vam pomoći?
Sorry, this is the only one.	Žao mi je, ovo je jedino
That's all I have.	To je sve što imam
There is no more.	Nema više
How much/many do you want?	Koliko želite?

153

| Will that be all? | Je li to sve? |
| Would you like anything else? | Želite li još nešto? |

On the shopping spree...

Bakery	pekara
Bank	banka
Barber/hairdresser	berber/frizer
Bookstore	knjižara
Pharmacy	apoteka
Clothes store	prodavnica konfekcije
Department store	robna kuća
Grocer	trgovac, prodavac
Market	trgovina
Newsstand	kiosk
Shoe store	prodavnica cipela
Travel agent	turistička agencija
Souvenir shop	prodavnica suvenira

Things to buy...

Book	knjiga
Carpet	čilim
Clock	sahat, časovnik
Coffee set	servis za kafu
Haircut	šišati
Handicrafts	zanat
Jewelry	nakit
Magazines	magacin, skladište
Map	mapa, karta
Paper	arak papir
Pen/pencil	pero - olovka
Postcards	razglednica
Pottery	lončarstvo

Clothing

The traditional outfit worn by Muslim women is called "dimije" and is a beautiful flowing trouser made of one

154

very large pant leg that has two elasticized holes for the
feet. Usually made of bright colors, it is only worn by
people from the village. I think it could catch on in
windy places!

Bag	torba
Belt	pojas, kaiš
Boots	čizme
Dress	odijelo, haljine
Coat	ogrtač
Gloves	rukavice
Hat	kapa
Jacket	jakna
Jeans	teksas (!) , đins
Pocket	džep
Scarf	marama, šal
Shirt	košulja muška
Shoes	cipele
Socks	čarape
Suit	odijelo
Sweater	džemper
Tie	kravata
Trousers	platnene pantalone
Umbrella	kišobran

Toiletries

aspirin	aspirin, prašak
Band-Aid	flaster, hanzaplast
brush	četka za kosu
comb	češalj
condom	prezervativ
deodorant	dezodorans
razor	britva
shampoo	šampon
shaving cream	krema za brijanje
soap	sapun
sunscreen	krema za sunčanje

tissues	maramice
toilet paper	toalet papir
toothbrush	četkica za zube
toothpaste	pasta za zube

Descriptions

cotton	pamuk
leather	uštavljena koža
modern	moderan
silk	svila
stone	kamen, zrno
traditional	tradicionalan
wood	šuma, drvo
wool	vuna

Photography

How much is it to process this	Koliko košta film? razvijanje filma?
When will it be ready?	Kada će biti gotovo?
I need film for this camera.	Ja želim film za ovu kameru
battery	baterija
B & W film	crno-bijeli film
color film	film u boji
flash	blic
lens	sočivo
photograph	slika

Electrical items

adaptor	ispravljač, adapter
cassette player	kasetofon
cassette tape	kaseta
fan	ventilator
hairdryer	fen za kosu
radio	radio

Emergency

Help!	U pomoć!
Could you help me please?	Možete li mi pomoći, molim?
Can I use your telephone?	Mogu li se poslužiti vašim telefonom?
Where is the nearest telephone?	Gdje je najbliži telefon?
Does the phone work?	Da li telefon radi?
Get help quickly!	Pozovi pomoć brzo!
Call the police!/doctor!/ ambulance!	Zovi policiju / doktora / hitnu!
I'll call the police!	Ja ču zvati policiju!
Is there a doctor near here?	Ima li negdje blizu doktor?
I'll get medical help!	Ja ču pozvati medicinsku pomoć!
There's been an accident!	Bio je sudar!
Is anyone hurt?	Da li je neko povrijeđen?
This person is hurt	Ova osoba je povrijeđena.
There are people injured	Ima povrijeđenih.
Don't move!	Ne mići se!
This is an emergency!	Ovo je hitan slučaj!
Go away!	Idi odavde!
I am ill	Ja sam bolestan.
I've been raped	Ja sam silovana
Take me to a doctor	Odvedi me doktoru.
I've been robbed!	Ja sam opljačkan!
Thief!	Lopov!
My...has been stolen!	Moj... je ukraden.
I've lost my...	Izgubio sam moje....

bags	torbe
camera equipment	opremu za kameru
handbag	ručnu torbu
money	novac, pare
passport	pasoš
traveler's checks	putne čekove
wallet	novčanik
My possessions are insured	Moje stvari su osigurane
I have a problem	Ja imam problem
I didn't do it	Ja nisam to uradio/-la
I'm sorry	Žao mi je
I apologize	Izvinjavam se, Izvinite
I want to contact my embassy	Ja želim kontaktirati ambasadu
I speak English	Ja govorim Engleski
I need an interpreter	Ja trebam prevodioca
Is it safe?	Je li sigurno?
Show me.	Pokaži mi.
clinic	klinika
doctor	doktor, ljekar
nurse	medicinska sestra, bolničarka
hospital	bolnica
policeman	milicioner, policajac
police station	policijska stanica

Healthcare

What's the matter?	U čemu je problem?
I am sick	Ja sam bolestan
My companion is sick	Moj priatelj je bolestan

May I see a female doctor?	Mogu li dobiti doktor*icu*?
I have medical insurance	Ja imam medicinsko osiguranje
Please undress	Molim svucite se.
How long have you had this problem?	Koliko dugo imate taj problem?
How long have you been feeling sick?	Koliko dugo vas boli?
Where does it hurt?	Gdje vas boli?
It hurts here.	Ovdje boli.
I've been vomiting	Ja sam povraćao
I feel dizzy	Ja osjećam vrtoglavicu
I can't eat/sleep	Ja ne mogu jesti / spavati
I feel worse/better	Osjećam se gore/ bolje
I am.../Are you...?	Ja sam... / Jeste li... ?
asthmatic	asmatičar
diabetic	dijabetičar
epileptic	epileptičar / padavičar
pregnant	trudna
I have... / You have...	Ja imam... / Vi imate...
a cold	prehladu
a cough	kašalj
a fever	groznicu
a fracture	prelom / frakturu
a headache	glavobolju
a heart condition	slabo srce
a sore throat	upalu grla
a stomachache	bolove u stomaku
a toothache	zubobolju
an allergy	alergiju
an infection	infekciju

an itch	svrab
constipation	zatvorenu stolicu
chest pain	bol u grudima
diarrhea	proljev

Medication	**Lijek**
I take this medication...	Ja uzimam ove lijekove.
I need medication for...	Ja trebam lijekove za...
What type of medication is this?	Koja vrsta lijekova je to?
How many times a day must I take it?	Koliko puta dnevno moram uzimati lijek?
When should I stop?	Kada trebam prestati?
I'm on antibiotics	Ja sam na antibioticima
I'm allergic to penicillin	Ja sam alergičan na pencilin
I've been vaccinated	Ja sam vakcinisan
Is it possible for me to travel?	Da li mogu putovati?
painkillers	lijek za ublažavanje bolova
tranquilizers	umirujuće sredstvo
drug	droga

Health words	
AIDS	SIDA
alcoholism	alkoholizam
amputation	amputacija
anemia	anemija
anesthetic	anestezija
blood	krv
blood group	krvna grupa
blood pressure	krvni pritisak
- low BP	- nizak k.p.

160

- high BP	- visok k.p.
bone	kost
cancer	rak
epidemic	epidemija
frostbite	ozeblina
hepatitis	hepatitis
indigestion	probavne smetnje
flu	gripa
pain	bol
rabies	bjesnilo
shrapnel	šrapnel, geler
snake bite	zmijski ugriz
surgeon	kirurg
torture	mučenje, tortura
transfusion	transfuzija

Eyesight

I've broken my glasses.	Ja sam slomio naočare.
Can you repair them?	Možete li ih popraviti?
I need new glasses.	Ja trebam nove naočare.
When can I pick them up?	Kada mogu doći po njih?
contact lenses	kontakne leće
contact lens solution	otopina za kontakne leće

Dangerous Situations

Stop!	Stop, Stani
Don't move!	Ne mrdaj!
Go!	Idi'
Who are you?	Ko ste vi?
Don't shoot!	Ne pucajte!
Keep quiet!	Budite mirni!

bomb	bomba
bullet	tane, zrno
disaster	nesreča, katastrofa
gun	revolver, pištolj
minefield	minsko polje
shell	granata
shrapnel	šrapnel
war	rat (fitting, I think)

Keeping Time

Seasons

summer	ljeto
autumn	jesen
winter	zima
spring	proljeće

Days of the Week

Monday	ponedjeljak
Tuesday	utorak
Wednesday	srijeda
Thursday	četvrtak
Friday	petak
Saturday	subota
Sunday	nedjelja

Months

January	januar
February	februar
March	mart
April	april
May	maj
June	juni
July	juli
August	august
September	septembar
October	oktobar
November	novembar
December	decembar

Times

century	vijek, stoljeće
decade	decenija
year	godina
month	mjesec

week	sedmica
day	dan
hour	sat, sahat
minute	minuta
second	sekunda
sunrise, dawn	zora, sabah
morning	jutro
noon	podne
afternoon	poslije podne
evening	veče
sunset	sumrak, akšam
night	noć
midnight	ponoć
today	danas
tomorrow	sutra
yesterday	juče
the day after tomorrow	prekosutra
the day before yesterday	prekjuče
last night	sinoć
tonight	večeras
this morning	jutros
yesterday morning	juče ujutro
yesterday afternoon	juče poslije podne
tomorrow morning	sutra ujutro
tomorrow afternoon	sutra poslije podne
tomorrow night	sutra naveće
this week/year	ove sedmice/godine
last week/year	prošle sedmice/godine
next week/year	iduće sedmice/godine
now	sada
past	prošlo
present	sadašnje
future	buduće

KEEPING TIME

What is today?	Koji je danas dan?
What is the date today?	Koji je danas datum?
What time is it?	Koliko je sati
It is ____ o'clock	Sada je _____ sati
almost	gotovo, skoro
ready	gotovo, yes it is!
already	već
always	uvijek
sometimes	ponekad
never	nikad
often	često

Numbers - Brojevi

0	nula
1	jedan
2	dva
3	tri
4	četiri
5	pet
6	šest
7	sedam
8	osam
9	devet
10	deset
11	jedanaest
12	dvanaest
13	trinaest
14	četrnaest
15	petnaest
16	šestnaest
17	sedamnaest
18	osamnaest
19	devetnaest
20	dvadeset
21	dvadeset i jedan
30	trideset
40	četrdeset
50	pedeset
60	šesdeset
70	sedamdeset
80	osamdeset
90	devedeset
100	sto, stotina
101	stotinu i jedan
1,000	hiljada
1,000,000	milion
1,000,000,000	milijarda

Ordinal Numbers

first	prvi
second	drugi
third	treći
fourth	četvrti
fifth	peti
sixth	šesti
seventh	sedmi
eighth	osmi
ninth	deveti
tenth	deseti

Other numbers

single	jednostruko
double	dvostruko
triple	trostruko
once	jedanput
twice	dvaput
thrice	triput
twice as much	dvaput toliko
once more	još jedom
first of all...	u prvom redu
secondly	u drugom redu
again	ponovo
last	konačan
half	jedna polovina, pola
quarter	jedna četvrtina, frtalj
point seven (.7)	nula zarez sedam

(Bosnians use a comma instead of a decimal point, and a point instead of a comma for separating 1 from 000 when writing 1,000)

You will hear the word "pola" used in telling time--
remember that it means "half way to" and not "half past"
or you will be an hour late all the time!
"pola osam" = 7:30, not half past 8:00!

168

Nations and Nationalities

Country	Jezik/Language	Države/Country	Državljani/Citizenship
Australia	-	Australija	Australac/Australka
Austria	-	Austrija	Austrijanac/Austrijanka
Belgium	-	Belgija	Belgijanac/Belgijanka
Bulgaria	bugarski	Bugarska	Bugar-in/ka
China	kineski	Kina	Kinez/ -kinja
Croatia	hrvatski	Hrvatska	Hrvat/ica
Czech Republic	češki	Češka	Čeh/inja
Denmark	danski	Danska	Dan-ac/kinja
England	engleski	Engleska	Englez/Engleskinja
Finland	finski	Finska	Fin-ac/kinja
France	francuski	Francuska	Francuz/kinja
Greece	grčki	Grčka	Grk/inja
Germany	njemečki	Njemačka	Nijemac/Nijemica
Holland	holandski	Nizozemska	Nizozem-ac/ka
Hungary	madžarski	Madžarska	Madžar/-ica
India	indijski	Indija	Indij-ac/ka
Italy	italijanski	Italija	Talijan/ka
Japan	japanski	Japan	Japan-ac/ka
Norway	norveški	Norveška	Norvežanin/ka
Poland	poljski	Poljska	Poljak/inja
Romania	rumunski	Rumunjska	Rumun-j/ka
Russia	ruski	Rusija	Rus/kinja
Serbia	srpski	Srbija	Srbin/Srbijanka
Slovakia	slovački	Slovačka	Slovak/inja
Slovenia	slovenski	Slovenija	Sloven-ac/ka
Spain	španjolski	Španjolska	Španjol-ac/ka
Sweden	švedski	Švedska	Šveđan-in/ka
Switzerland	-	Švicarska	Švicar-ac/kinja
Turkey	turski	Turska	Turčin/Turkinja
United States	-	Sjedinje Države	Amerikan-ac/ka

169

You can't expect me to think of everything!
So here are some...
Pages for Notes

Pages for Notes

Other Balkan Language Titles from Hippocrene ...

ALBANIAN-ENGLISH/ ENGLISH-ALBANIAN PRACTICAL DICTIONARY
400 pages • 4³/₈ x 7 • 18,000 entries •
0-7818-0419-1 • $14.95pb • (483)

ALBANIAN DICTIONARY AND PHRASEBOOK
2,000 entries • 200 pages • 3¾ x 7½ • $11.95pb
• 0-7818-0793-X • (498)

ALBANIAN PHRASEBOOK
245 pages • 3¾ x 7½ • $9.95pb •
0-7818-0791-3 • (106)

ENGLISH-ALBANIAN COMPREHENSIVE DICTIONARY
60,000 entries • 938 pages • 6 x 9½ • $60.00hc
• W except Albania • 0-7818-0510-4 • (615)

ENGLISH-ALBANIAN COMPREHENSIVE DICTIONARY
60,000 entries • 938 pages • 6 x 9 • $35.00pb •
W except Albania • 0-7818-0792-1 • (305)

ENGLISH-ALBANIAN DICTIONARY OF IDIOMS
524 pages • 5½ x 8½ • 0-7818-0783-2 •
$19.95pb • (219)

**BOSNIAN-ENGLISH/
ENGLISH-BOSNIAN
CONCISE DICTIONARY**
8,500 entries • 331 pages • 4 x 6 •
0-7818-0276-8 • $14.95pb • (329)

**BOSNIAN-ENGLISH/
ENGLISH-BOSNIAN
COMPACT DICTIONARY**
8,500 entries • 331 pages • 3¼ x 4¾ •
0-7818-0499-X • $8.95pb • (204)

**BOSNIAN-ENGLISH/
ENGLISH-BOSNIAN
DICTIONARY AND PHRASEBOOK**
1,500 entries • 171 pages • 3¾ x 7 •
0-7818-0596-1 • $11.95pb • (691)

**BULGARIAN-ENGLISH/
ENGLISH-BULGARIAN
COMPACT DICTIONARY**
8,000 entries • 322 pages • 0-7818-0535-X •
$8.95pb • (623)

**BULGARIAN-ENGLISH/
ENGLISH-BULGARIAN
PRACTICAL DICTIONARY**
8,000 entries • 323 pages • 4³/₈ x 7 •
0-87052-145-4 • $14.95pb • (331)

BEGINNER'S BULGARIAN
207 pages • 5½ x 8½ • 0-7818-0300-4 •
$9.95pb • (76)

MACEDONIAN-ENGLISH/ ENGLISH-MACEDONIAN CONCISE DICTIONARY
10,000 entries • 180 pages • 4 x 6 •
0-7818-0516-3 • $14.95pb • (619)

SERBIAN-ENGLISH/ ENGLISH-SERBIAN CONCISE DICTIONARY
7,500 entries • 394 pages • 4 x 6 •
0-7818-0556-2 • W • $14.95pb • (326)

SERBO-CROATIAN-ENGLISH/ ENGLISH-SERBO-CROATIAN PRACTICAL DICTIONARY
24,000 entries • 527 pages • 4 ½ x 7 •
0-7818-0445-0 • $16.95pb • (130)

SLOVENE-ENGLISH/ ENGLISH-SLOVENE MODERN DICTIONARY
36,000 entries • 935 pages • 4 ¼ x 7 •
0-7818-0252-0 • $24.95pb • (19)

Prices subject to change without prior notice. To order Hippocrene Books, contact your local bookstore, call (718) 454-2366, or write to: Hippocrene Books, 171 Madison Ave., New York, NY 10016. Please enclose check or money order adding $5.00 shipping (UPS) for the first book and $.50 for each additional title.

Printed in the USA
CPSIA information can be obtained
at www.ICGtesting.com
JSHW051413310823
47641JS00017B/61